Asleep

at the

Will

The Dormant Soul Complex

ISBN: 979-8-9999455-3-2 (Hardcover)

ISBN: 979-8-9999455-4-9 (Paperback)

ISBN: 979-8-9999455-5-6 (Ebook)

Asleep at the Will | The Dormant Soul Complex
by Etmol Roman Clynegove

Contents

Introduction

AI Disclosure

Authors writing books before 1868 would've had reservations about writers in 1870 using typewriters. Writers accustomed to using typewriters would've cast a raised eyebrow toward authors after 1976 who chose to use a word processor. Artificial Intelligence is another even greater evolution; another opportunity to ask "is it the tool or the human using the tool?" I empathize with the concern. A typewriter or a word processor couldn't generate a term paper on the work of Tolkien, using the writing style of Stephen King in under 8 minutes. Writing, as it has always been, is about communicating, exploring, and expressing one's unique perspectives and concepts.

The concepts and core insights that are the basis for this book emerged from the author's own observations and experiences. In the interest of transparency and integrity, AI was used as a tool for this work in the following ways:

- **Historical validation and research access:** To validate historical patterns and specific dates or eras, and access qualitative and quantitative research data. The insights, concepts, and perspectives on human history or existing historical research originated with the writer. AI assisted in ascertaining specific dates, times, eras, and particular historical events, as well as accessing academic/scholarly research. However, all AI-generated responses were source checked and validated through additional manual research by the writer.

- **Analyzing patterns and themes:** This work, in its original form, was several years of the writer's handwritten journals. Those pages were scanned, converted to text, and then edited and refined manually. Those entries were then manually grouped according to the writer's own tags and themes. AI was utilized as a secondary step to analyze those tags and themes collectively. The writer manually reviewed and edited this analysis, allowing it to influence the organizational structure without replacing the writer's original framework.

- **Conversational development:** A significant amount of time was spent speaking parts of this work as it evolved. AI was used conversationally to 'discuss' concepts and insights as they emerged for the purpose of mirroring them back to the writer. AI was tasked with converting the resulting recordings to text. That text was then manually copyedited. AI was used to check the spelling and grammar of text from these conversations.

- **'Debating' the concepts:** Several of the concepts in this work were 'debated' using AI, prompting it to 'act as': 'a 71-year-old Jungian analyst who is averse to technology,' 'a 26-year-old social media influencer and activist,' 'a busy mother of two with a corporate job who practices yoga and goes to a couple of wellness retreats a year'—and then asking those personae to participate in debates or discussions. These virtual debates helped stress-test ideas and identify potential counterarguments. When AI 'asked' clarifying questions or 'requested' elaboration, the writer evaluated whether such prompts helped articulate existing thoughts more clearly or differently. However, all substantive responses and conceptual developments came from the writer's own human reflection and analysis. These 'debates' helped refine the expression of existing ideas but didn't materially alter the work's core concepts, arguments, or conclusions.

- **Simplification of concepts:** Some of the lofty/verbose/complex/abstract ideas were debated and discussed with AI. The writer considered the 'conversations' introspectively, as a curious human thinker. The initial concept was occasionally refined, ensuring that its core, essential message was intact and not compromised - and only then ratified and included.

The fundamental concept, framework, insights, and arguments presented in this work remain entirely the intellectual property and creative output of the writer. AI served as a research and organizational tool, not as a creative collaborator, ghostwriter, or co-author.

Preface

by Etmol Roman Clynegove

This is not a manifesto. It is intended to be a mirror.

It is not a dogma. It is meant to be a tool.

The work that follows names a condition I have observed, wrestled with, and, at times embodied… yet struggled to name. I've listened to many other loved ones, friends and peers talk around this condition without quite being able to name it. What I offer here is a name, *'dormant soul complex'*, and acknowledge that it may raise more questions than answers. This is a personal conceptual framework - not the product of clinical or academic research. This is not an ontological debate, it's meant to be an applied conceptual framework. You don't have to be Jungian to engage with this work, his key concepts will be explained along the way. If this work resonates for you then it is for you.

This framework has been quietly emerging for nearly three decades. I was first exposed to Jung early in my higher-learning career. His work immediately resonated for me. It was interesting information and I developed a certain degree of knowledge about his theories. It wasn't until about ten years ago— after I'd grappled with complexes, danced with my shadows, and inflated then deflated my ego more than a few times—that my knowledge of Jung alchemized with my lived life and began emerging as something that may be akin to wisdom. Individuation is ongoing. This framework has been patiently waiting. My Critic says it'll never be complete enough or refined enough to share. My daimon shouts "what are you waiting for?" …it's a good thing we're all friends… at least most of the time.

I write under a pseudonym because I believe the work matters more than who wrote it. It also helps to distance my ego from the work.

What you encounter in these pages might challenge you. It might serve you, or it might not. Take what's useful and leave the rest.

—*E.R.C.*

Foreword

Dreams strip us of autonomy. In the dreamscape, actions and reactions don't originate from the Self; we have no actual agency—no matter how real the dream seems.

Much like our current age. The great human soul isn't just sleeping—it's 'asleep at the will.' Sovereignty lost, we drift, in stupor, on a churning river of distraction.

We're overwhelmed by the spectacle of performative politics and the theatrics of manufactured outrage. We're seduced by the unfulfillable promises of capitalism. Deceived by staged religion and commodified spiritual awakenings, we're sung lullabies by pop-culture gurus. Lost in the curated mirages of social media 'friends' we follow but have never met. Enraged by words and language, yet impotently unresponsive to egregious actions. Intellectually glutted, while wisdom withers away. We drown in a deluge of information utterly devoid of meaning—piped into our echo chambers by insidious algorithms built from conversations overheard by our ever-present devices.

We've excelled at becoming compulsive consumers, vengeful voters, influential influencers, servile corporate supplicants. But the very human drives to choose, to aspire, to create seem dormant still. Fulfillment always *just* beyond reach. Our digital footprints are worth more than our souls.

For over 5,000 years we've been evolving toward our current iteration of extractive systems. It is not inherently evil or malicious, it's functioning as designed—either intentionally or by unconscious evolution.

Maybe it's time to ask: even when we get the degree, the spouse/partner/ lover, the job, the house… why do we still carry the persistent, unyielding *quiet disquiet* malaise in our very core? Why does it bother us only if we get still for too long? What's missing when we already have it all?

My Process

I write from liminal spaces, quiet pauses between certainties—uncomfortable places where honest conversations actually happen. The place where polarities exist and are held together in tension. Conversations that rush, then crawl, with disrupted cadence. Uneven rhythms. Irregular inhales and exhales. Not because I've transcended ideological thinking, but because I've found myself between camps that each hold fragments of detail... fragments that *feel true* while bypassing the essential truths born from the myths that bind all the fragments together.

This work came primarily from self-observation. I'm fascinated by still, shadowed places where real change occurs and the soul awakens—not in performative public spaces, but rather in those moments when we encounter ourselves without pretense. Those periods that feel like nearly-catastrophic breakdowns that are transformed by deep introspection into breakthroughs. When our naked emperors finally tire of others fawning over their clothing. I watch human patterns of life like weather systems: we create our own storms, then seek shelter, navigating through fog by barely visible stars and eclipsed moons.

My storytellers came from many different realms, but they all understood the nature of the hidden sparks and shadows inside us: Jung taught me how to initiate myself into my Self. Campbell helped me connect my Self to the myths humans have always told. Von Franz, Shaw, Meade, and Bly helped me see the mythological narratives playing out in my ordinary life. Hillman, Kalsched, and Woodman helped me transform my lead into gold. Whitman, Blake, and Coelho inducted me into love of the mystery and awe for the riddle. Kierkegaard, Nietzsche, de Beauvoir, Foucault, Bloch, and Heidegger helped me grapple with the profound freedom and overwhelming responsibility of being human.

Then the contemporary narrators: Esther Perel, John Vervaeke, Bell Hooks, Robert A. Johnson, Murray Stein, Gabor Maté, Bessel van der Kolk. Each one illuminated something different or told another part of the story of how we work as humans and how we function socially.

I carry my own biases and they'll certainly affect this conversation; some are known and some are unknown. I'll name the ones that surface in this framework: I'm suspicious of systems that concentrate power while promising liberation. I'm drawn to individual agency, but wary of individualism that abandons personal responsibility. I value psychological insight but distrust simplistic therapeutic approaches that avoid mundane realities. I'm indoctrinated from birth as a Westerner; an American. Rather than pretending objectivity, I use my particular way of seeing as a deliberate tool, transparent in the work. I'm not asking you to adopt my view, but inviting you to use it as a mirror for discovering your own.

I challenge conventions not from cynicism but from hope. When I interrogate false idols, like the myth of perfect objectivity, addiction to external validation, the comfort of victimhood, blind faith in extractive systems—I do so because destroying constructs that don't serve us creates space for generative solutions that can lead to a thriving collective. This is critical inquiry in service of possibility.

What drives this work is the journey toward Eudaimonic Sovereignty— deep inner authority that comes from knowing yourself, understanding your own patterns, and choosing conscious responses instead of automatic reactions. I'm interested in how we become complicit in our own limitations, how we internalize external systems of extraction and control, how we can recognize and interrupt those patterns, and what becomes possible when we operate from genuine choice rather than conditioned reaction.

I write as someone engaged in the lifelong work of becoming the author of my own story rather than a character in someone else's. But I write from the middle of that work, not from its completion. My hope is that this exploration serves as both mirror and invitation—helping others recognize their own capacity for authentic choice and the courage to claim it.

Along the way, I've been fortunate enough to 'sit at the campfire' with two noteworthy explorers: Danielle A. and Jason W. Our conversations crystalized many of my thoughts into language that could be shared, mirrored, and held lightly. I'm not sure this work would've ever been grounded or refined enough to write without the two of them.

The questions that drive this work are deceptively simple: How do we become who we actually are? How do we heal without bypassing difficult truths? How do we live in contemporary society without losing ourselves? How do we build a world that honors both individual sovereignty and collective responsibility?

I don't offer final answers because the questions that matter most resist easy resolution. Instead, I offer open inquiry, careful observation, and the perspective of someone else walking the path—someone who believes our greatest freedom lies not in escaping the human condition, but in learning to inhabit it more fully.

Ask the question, but live the answer. Seek the journey, not the destination ...*for that is life.*

Primary Influences

I have many influences, but the two biggest for this framework are Jung and Marx. There's an alchemical aspect of the tension between their seemingly divergent contributions. Marx shaped my understanding of material systems, power structures, and human alienation, illuminating the sociocultural exterior. Jung, conversely, provided the conceptual grounding for the interior self and its intricate dance with civilization's apparatus. When tensions arose between these frameworks, I reconciled them by focusing on their psychological or psychospiritual implications. The human Self was given authority as the ultimate arbiter.

This attempt of creating a synthesis between Jung and Marx is not new and not uniquely my own. In particular, Julien-François Gerber's *'Karl with Carl: Marxism and the Jungian Path to the Soul'* was published in 2022 in the *International Journal of Jungian Studies*, Volume 14, Issue 2. Gerber explicitly aims to bring these two thinkers together to address human flourishing and emancipation, bridging the social/individual, conscious/unconscious, and material/spiritual dimensions. Gerber argues that a Jungian approach can uniquely contribute the "notion of the soul," a "positive view of the unconscious and its potentials," and an "opening to spirituality" to critical theory.

Lewis Mumford and Theodore Roszak, both notably, in their distinct ways, drew upon and implicitly or explicitly resonated with elements of Marxist and Jungian thought in the development of their critiques of industrial society. Their thinking has contributed greatly to the contemporary degrowth discourse.

Beyond Jung and Marx, there is a diverse group of other direct and indirect influences, including Thomas Singer and Samuel Kimbles, Joseph Henderson, Arthur Koestler, Shoshana Zuboff, and even The Frankfurt School (the Institute for Social Research, German: *Institut für Sozialforschung*), in spite of their sharp criticisms of Jung. There have been so many more; I'll include them in my bibliography.

My personal observations and the resulting conceptual framework are both more Jungian in tone. They tend to focus more on the psychospiritual core of humans and human flourishing. I offer the analytical framework mostly as an artifact - it is the map I used to navigate the bidirectional relationship between the interior of the psyche and the sociocultural exterior world. On that bidirectional road is where I first encountered the psychic patterns that later became the Dormant Soul Complex (DSC). At its root, DSC is a psychological concept. It emerged from ongoing internal conversations with Jungian concepts. It is not official, nor sanctioned—it is a name that I use to talk about a recurring persistent pattern.

The Conceptual Framework

The core of this framework is quite simple, I contend that:

Many find our contemporary, extractive way of life unfulfilling most of the time.

The psyche has developed a complex in response to that pervasive hollowness of life.

We, as humans, can address that complex through individuation.

Once humans begin individuation, they and others who've done the same, can collectively build something more generative for everyone.

My vision for a path forward may be labeled by some as utopian or unrealistic; my analytical framework may be considered too broad or too multidisciplinary. But for me, this is more speculative social philosophy, what can we do collectively if we work toward building a generative/regenerative society? The future I posit may be utopian or too far-sighted, but it is differentiated by its organic, decentralized, and emergent nature as a counterpoint to planned utopias. It's simply one perspective on how we move forward.

Through the analytic lens of this framework I've observed:

We live in an extractive civilization. Most contemporary systems and subsystems are somehow extractive—explicitly or implicitly; occasionally or relentlessly. Some systems and subsystems are more extractive than others; some are tolerably extractive and others detrimentally extractive.

Since the Bronze Age we've built civilizations that tend to be extractive, either by intentional design or unconscious evolution, by force or by coercion. Even with the best intentions, the collective shadow emerges enabling extraction. Extraction seems to be an inherent aspect of our sociocultural apparatus and psychological blueprint, expressed through the collective shadow. It isn't merely *capitalism* versus *socialism*—extraction appears to be endemic. Socialism would likely become extractive if implemented without resolution of the collective shadow.

Our systems are organized through sophisticated interrelationships between Extractive System hosts and Paraextractive and Subextractive subordinate systems. These systems express across a wide range of smaller sociocultural facets of civilization. This complexity provides the collective shadow a nearly infinite number of vectors to influence or override the individual shadow. To further complicate the functionality of these systems, they are not static nor fixed; they have variable degrees of extractiveness. They're not *always* extractive; they aren't *only* extractive; they're not even *obviously* extractive. Systems can be *slightly* extractive, *occasionally* extractive, or *selectively* extractive, or *unevenly* extractive, or *heterogeneously* extractive. Yet in some way, shape, or form they are extractive. The cumulative impact of these layered extractive systems profoundly affects our individual psyches, creating an ecosystem of extraction.

The impact of ubiquitous extraction across our web of systems and sociocultural facets culminates as a condition called the 'dormant soul complex'. This complex emerges through a syntonic relationship between the collective shadow and the individual shadow. The Dormant Soul Complex expresses as an internalized predisposition toward being extracted from, and a general dormancy of vital psychic energy. We become complicit *in* and susceptible *to* further extraction—our will subdued and our agency compromised. The DSC may be resolved through Jung's individuation process.

Individuation, I concur would transform the individual's relationship to their own shadow, thereby weakening the collective shadow's influence. Though individuation is a lifelong pursuit, I posit that through the process of individuation one develops Eudaimonic Sovereignty. Eudaimonic Sovereignty enables the Self to identify and then mitigate or disengage from extractive systems. Those sovereign individuals, I propose, have the potential to create a generative/regenerative society.

Once an individual develops Eudaimonic Sovereignty they're posited to seek relationships with other individuals who are also developing Eudaimonic Sovereignty. Through Koinonic Syntonomy those individuals form small, collective, mutually-beneficial groups that are more generative/regenerative. Those groups organically evolve into a larger societal generative/regenerative infrastructure through Autonomic Synergeia.

I surmise that a peaceful revolution of Eudaimonically Sovereign individuals would form Koinonically Syntonomic groups. These groups would further organize into an Autonomically Synergistic infrastructure that would transition power and energy away from extractive systems and into generative/regenerative systems.

Part I |
Extractive Systems

The systems we exist in

Extraction is subtle. It's built in. It's nearly invisible. It is ingrained, even anticipated.

Just Last Week

- It's 4:15 PM on Tuesday afternoon. Your boss sends an urgent email, telling you that even though your monthly report is due on Friday. The CEO wants it by tomorrow; there's no reason - the CEO just wants to see it. Your heart rate increases. Your blood pressure rises... Uuggghhhh... not again... your daughter has soccer practice in 45 minutes. It's either finish and send the report to your boss or take her to practice. Without thinking twice you text to tell her that she'll have to get another ride to practice. This happens frequently enough that you almost expect it... so does she.

- You get a text from a friend. It is an invite for dinner. You decide to go, knowing that you'll probably be expected to pick up the check, as usual, because you make significantly more money. You were roommates in college, and even though that was several years ago, you still anticipate feeling guilty if you opt out. It bothers you, just not enough to bring it up.

- You get invited to a wedding by an old friend you haven't seen in many years. You 'see' each other on social media; you text occasionally. But you haven't hung out together in about 5 years. Turns out, it is a destination wedding, in Ireland. She texts you and asks where your RSVP is. You don't really want to go, and financially speaking, it'll have to go on your credit card. You can't really say "no" can you?

- You receive an email from a prestigious university. You're invited to be a speaker at their next symposium on AI. It would be an honor to be on the panel. It's a big deal. You get excited. You click to register and it appears that there's a fee, for you to participate. Your expertise, credibility, and intellectual capital are being exchanged for prestige. They're really asking you pay to contribute to their event's value? Is it worth it?

- You finish your 50 page paper on Symbology in Renaissance Art. You have meticulously researched all of your sources. You've crafted a well written document. You're even proud of it; it's your first big paper of the semester. Your professor was clear at the beginning of the semester that the university was implementing AI-detection from a widely accepted company that purports to be very accurate in the academic space. You PDF your paper and upload it to the AI-detector. It looks like your paper is '86% AI-generated' with a '74% confidence level.' That can't be right... you wrote this paper. You intentionally didn't use AI for anything; you spent the last 3 weeks on research and properly formatting all your citations and footnotes. What now?

Think things were different in the good old days? ...think again.

It's not just modern life. It's not just *your* particular life. It's not you. Extraction has been a systemic part of our civilization since at least the Bronze Age—from the Bronze Age to that last text you got from your boss; it's a pattern.

A Brief History of Extraction

Bronze Age (3300-1200 BCE)

Bronze Age civilizations developed diverse methods for acquiring resources and expanding territory. Most societies relied on palace economy systems that concentrated agricultural surplus and trade wealth in centralized bureaucracies before redistributing primarily to elites and palace officials. While some empires like Assyria used military conquest to extract wealth and labor, others such as the Indus Valley civilization emphasized trade networks. Most combined warfare with diplomacy and commerce, establishing multiple models for state expansion beyond organized violence alone.

Human roles

- You're a skilled artisan, hammering out beautiful bronze tools and weapons for the city-state's elite. You live and work within the palace compound, fed and housed, but the raw copper and tin are brought from distant mines by laborers, who rarely see the finished products or benefit from the trade you facilitate.

- Your village sits near the river, and its fertile banks yield plentiful grain. When the annual floods come, the temple priests, who control the vast granaries, demand a significant portion of your harvest as an offering to the gods. You give it, knowing their stored surplus is the only thing that keeps everyone from starving in lean years, and they control who gets how much.

- You're a farmer, living a simple life on the fringes of a growing empire. Suddenly, armed men arrive, demanding a tribute of livestock and young men for the distant capital's armies. They don't offer much in return, just the unspoken threat of violence if you refuse.

Iron Age (1200-500 BCE)

The major focus of emerging empires and city-states was developing taxation and bureaucratic systems to keep their armies funded and trained, which allowed dominant powers to control vast territories and populations. This era saw multiple civilizations - including the Assyrian, Persian, Neo-Babylonian, and Egyptian empires, as well as Greek city-states and Chinese dynasties - independently develop sophisticated administrative systems to systematically extract wealth from populations through taxation, tribute, and forced labor. These innovations in statecraft and resource extraction became foundational models for imperial administration that would influence governance structures for millennia.

Human roles

- You're a metalworker, using the new, harder iron to forge tools and weapons. A local chieftain demands a regular quota of your finest axes and swords, which he then trades to gain influence and power in the region. You're paid, but barely enough to feed your family, and refusing isn't an option.

- Your clan has traditionally hunted and gathered in these forests for generations. Now, a larger, more organized kingdom is expanding its borders, sending soldiers to patrol. They restrict your access to prime hunting grounds and demand a portion of your catch to support their growing population centers, threatening to settle their own people on your land if you don't comply.

- You're a member of a conquered tribe. Your land has been taken, and now you're forced to work in the fields or mines under the watchful eyes of the conquerors. You receive basic rations, but the vast majority of your labor's output goes to feed and enrich the ruling class, who now live in the former homes of your elders.

Imperial Age - e.g., Roman, Persian, Hellenistic (500 BCE-500 CE)

Imperial powers developed sophisticated systems to extract wealth from conquered territories through taxation, tribute, and resource exploitation. While heavy taxation sometimes contributed to unrest and provincial revolts, successful empires like Rome and Persia balanced extraction with providing infrastructure, legal systems, and trade protection that legitimized their rule. Different imperial models emerged - from the Persian satrap system to Roman provincial administration to Chinese Han bureaucracy - each refining methods of long-distance control and wealth concentration.

Human roles

- You're a farmer in a distant province of a vast empire. Each year, imperial tax collectors arrive, demanding a heavy portion of your grain and livestock to feed the distant legions and the citizens of the capital city. They don't provide much direct benefit in return, but the absence of their legions might mean your village is plundered by barbarians.

- You're a talented artisan, captured in a recent war. You are now a slave in a wealthy Roman villa, crafting intricate mosaics and sculptures for your master's estate. Your artistic skill and labor are entirely owned by your master, with no compensation beyond basic sustenance, and your freedom is gone.

- You are a merchant, trading goods along established imperial routes. You face numerous tolls, tariffs, and bribes demanded by local governors and imperial officials at every checkpoint. These unofficial 'fees' reduce your profits, but they are the unspoken cost of doing business and navigating the empire's vast territory.

For the purpose of focus, these historical examples will shift toward Western culture.

Medieval Feudalism & Guild Era (500-1500 CE)

Feudalism institutionalized extraction through land ownership. Peasants provided labor and tribute to lords in exchange for 'protection.' Urban guilds emerged as a secondary nearly-equal system only nominally deferring to the lords. Guilds controlled craft production and trade while providing mutual protection for artisans and merchants. Though guilds operated with autonomy in cities, they remained subject to feudal lords through taxation and charters. Over time, powerful guild cities accumulated enough wealth to challenge traditional feudal authority, creating tensions between urban commercial power and rural landed nobility.

Human roles

- You're a peasant, bound to the land you work. Your lord provides a small plot for your family and theoretical protection, but you owe him days of labor on his fields (corvée), a portion of your harvest, and fees for using his mill or oven. You feel stuck; leaving means starvation or becoming a bandit.

- You're a young apprentice in a bustling medieval guild. You dedicate years to learning your craft, working long hours for little pay, often living with your master. You gain skills, but your labor directly enriches the master, and the guild controls your path to becoming independent, demanding loyalty and adherence to its strict rules.

- You're a minor noble, loyal to a powerful duke. The duke demands your military service, your knights, and a portion of the taxes you collect from your own meager lands whenever he rides to war or needs funds. You comply, knowing your own status and security depend entirely on his continued favor and protection.

Colonial Age (1500-1800 CE)

European powers established colonies as sources of raw materials and captive markets for finished products. Colonial territories were systematically prevented from manufacturing or trading with foreign powers to maximize extraction for mercantilist home countries. This period globalized extraction through colonial systems that stripped resources—including enslaved humans—from the Americas, Africa, and Asia to fuel European economic development and capital accumulation.

Human roles

- You are an Indigenous person living on ancestral lands now claimed by a European colonial power. You're forced to abandon traditional farming practices and cultivate cash crops like sugar or tobacco for export back to the mother country. You see little of the vast wealth generated, and your land is increasingly controlled by distant powers.

- You are a local craftsman in a colonial port city. Your traditional methods are being undercut by cheaper, mass-produced goods imported from the colonizing power. You're told this is progress, but your livelihood shrinks, and your skills become less valued in a market designed to benefit foreign industries.

- You are an enslaved African. You have been forcibly taken from your homeland and family, enduring the horrific journey across the Atlantic. Now, you labor under brutal conditions on a sugar or tobacco plantation. Your work is unceasing, and you are considered property, not a person. The wealth you generate through your forced labor is enjoyed entirely by the plantation owner and the colonial economy, while you live in constant fear and have no control over your life or future. Your culture and identity are suppressed, and the bonds of community are all that keep hope alive.

- You are a young man in a newly colonized territory. Each year, colonial officials arrive, demanding that your community provide a quota of men for labor on distant infrastructure projects or for military service in the colonial army. There is no direct pay; your participation is framed as a 'civic duty' to the new administration, even though it takes you from your family, community, and traditions for long periods.

- You are a local trader in a colonial port city. You're restricted by mercantilist laws, forced to buy and sell only from the ships and merchants of the colonizing power. You pay heavy duties on all goods, ensuring that the wealth from trade flows primarily back to the European metropolis, limiting your own economic growth.

Industrial & Capitalist Age (1800-1950 CE)

Industrial capitalism established sophisticated new systems of extraction, primarily through the commodification of labor and the accumulation of capital. Factory systems and mass production transformed human time and effort into wage labor, stripping producers of direct control over their work and its value, turning human life itself into a commodity. This era was characterized by an unprecedented concentration of wealth in the hands of industrialists and financiers, fueled by the relentless demand for raw materials, the expansion of global markets, and the instrumentalization of labor. Extraction in this age extended beyond physical resources to encompass the systematic appropriation of human time, productivity, and well-being through rigorous factory discipline, long working hours, and debt cycles.

Human roles

- You're a factory worker, toiling for 12 hours a day in dangerous, unsanitary conditions for a meager wage. A significant portion of your pay is lost to rent in company-owned housing or inflated prices at the company store, trapping you in a cycle of debt and dependency with your employer.

- You are a small farmer whose family has worked the land for generations. The expansion of railroads and powerful corporations means you can no longer compete; you're forced to sell your land for a pittance to a larger agricultural trust that then monocrops the entire region. They're amassing massive profits while you join the urban poor.

- You are a sharecropper in the American South after the Civil War. You're 'given' a small plot of land by a landowner, along with seeds and tools, in exchange for a large share of your cotton harvest. Year after year, despite your hard labor, the accounting for the land, tools, and supplies always leaves you in debt to the landowner, binding you to the land with no real path to economic independence.

- You are a young migrant worker, brought to a new country by promises of opportunity. You work in sweatshops or mines for long hours, paid far below minimum wage, and live in overcrowded, substandard housing controlled by your employer. Your labor fuels the rapid industrial growth, but your precarious legal status and language barrier prevent you from demanding fair treatment.

- You are a coal miner in the early 20th century. You descend deep into the earth daily, digging vast quantities of coal from dangerous, unstable seams. Your wages are barely enough to support your family, and you often find yourself paying for company-provided tools, housing, and even medical care, ensuring that most of the value you dig from the ground cycles back to the mine owner rather than to you.

Information Age (1950-Present)

This era sees the evolution of capitalist extraction, moving beyond primarily physical resources and labor to encompass increasingly sophisticated forms. Corporations and bureaucratic systems, operating in unison, continue to exert significant control over traditional industries and global supply chains, often leveraging financial instruments and globalized production networks to maximize capital accumulation. However, a defining feature of this age is the expansion of extraction into psychological and spiritual realms, particularly amplified by the digital revolution.

Modern extraction now also commodifies information and farms human attention, authentic development, and personal agency itself through hyperconnection, sophisticated invasive systems of digital distraction, and the pervasive collection and analysis of personal data. This dual evolution reflects a period where established capitalist mechanisms intersect with new forms of digital and cognitive exploitation.

Human roles

- You're a homeowner in the 1957. Developers are buying up land for new suburban subdivisions, promising modern conveniences and a better life. You're pressured to sell your older home in the city, for a lower price than its true value, as public services shift to the suburbs, effectively sacrificing your property value and community ties to fuel the expansion of a new housing market.

- It's 1965. You're a young professional, and to climb the corporate ladder, you're expected to spend evenings entertaining clients and weekends playing golf with your superiors. These social obligations are never explicitly required or compensated, but you know your personal time and social capital are expected as the unwritten cost of career advancement.

- You're a working mother in the 1974, juggling your full-time job with household responsibilities. Advertisements constantly tell you that a 'good mother' also provides homemade meals and a spotless home, subtly consuming your time and energy to meet ever-higher, unpaid domestic labor standards, often on top of your paid work.

- It's 1987. You've worked at the same manufacturing company for 25 years, always trusting you'd have a pension. Now, a corporate takeover means your plant is closing, and your pension fund has been 'restructured,' leaving you with a fraction of what you expected after decades of your labor contributed to the company's growth.

- You're a consumer in 1998. You sign up for a 'free' dial-up internet service, but to access it, you have to consent to a barrage of pop-up ads and allow the service to track your Browse habits, which are then sold to advertisers. Your attention and data are captured as the price of 'free' access.

- You're a recent college graduate in 2010. The job market has collapsed, but unpaid internships are everywhere, promising 'valuable experience' and potential full-time opportunities. You work 40+ hours a week without pay at a media company, essentially doing entry-level employee work. The media company extracts free skilled labor by leveraging your desperation for job in a recession.

- You're a content creator in a niche hobby. You feel constant pressure to produce content to feed an algorithm for diminishing returns. You're only making a small portion of what the platform is generating from your channel. Your hobby, time, and creativity are being monetized to generate ad revenue.

- You are on a social media app, it's 11:30 PM, you're restlessly scrolling endlessly, feeling anxious comparing yourself and your life to curated feeds. In the background your personal data is being logged for targeted advertising.

- You're a gig worker unable to make ends meet despite working long hours. You wanted independence but between the platforms taking such a large cut and paying for your own healthcare - you're working more than you did when you were corporate.

- You just switched to a new 'online only' bank. You're reviewing your first statement - you don't remember all those transaction fees they are charging... maybe they were mentioned somewhere in the thirty screens you scanned through during the 'quick and easy' account opening process.

- You're trying to resolve a billing error with your health insurance company. You spend hours on hold, get bounced between departments, and finally land with a customer service bot that just cycles through pre-programmed responses, offering no real solution. Your time, energy, and emotional well-being are subtly drained by the complex, impersonal system, leaving you frustrated and without resolution and the unpaid claim—one more claim that the company won't have to pay out.

- You're feeling overwhelmed and anxious. Advertisements pop up for apps promising 'instant mindfulness' or online courses for 'finding your inner peace,' all for a monthly fee. You see influencers promoting specific self-care apps as the key to happiness. Your genuine need for mental peace and spiritual well-being is being commodified, replaced by subscriptions and products rather than authentic internal work.

Extractive Systems Defined

What does 'extractive' really mean? …especially in regard to something as large as a civilization or something as small as me engaging with a text message?

Extractive

Extraction and *exploitation* have been pervasive influences throughout human civilization. For nearly as long, theories about these forces have emerged as conceptual frameworks across diverse disciplines including philosophy, critical theory, social analysis, financial studies, anthropology, cultural studies, social work, psychology, and technology studies.

In my conceptual framework, the choice to use *extractive* rather than *exploitative* is intentional. It provides semantic precision. *Extractive* could be seen as *exploitative; exploitative* could be seen as *extractive*. In my framework the nuance lies in the implied intent of the action.

The intent of an *extractive* action is ethically and morally ambiguous whereas the intent of an *exploitative* action is inherently unfair, unethical, or immoral. *Exploitative* would also intrinsically be *extractive*. *Extractive* focuses ambivalently on the act itself while *exploitative* infers deliberate harmful intent or callous disregard behind the act. While *extractive* is still critical, this nuance allows us to reference actions or systems with greater emotional neutrality while avoiding an implied vilification.

Defining Extractive Systems

Determining whether a system, method, or relationship is 'extractive' is a multifaceted inquiry. It necessitates a nuanced approach accounting for varying degrees and temporal variability. The observer's vantage point shapes the assessment of a system's extractiveness—is the observer inside the system or outside of it?—if they're inside, where are they in the hierarchy? At its core, an extractive system disproportionately siphons resources, value, or energy (physical or psychic) from its participants to another part of the system. Generally, this concentrates benefits upwards through the hierarchy, often with variable impacts on those from whom the extraction occurs, rendering the system, or aspects of it, partially or wholly extractive.

The Degree and Variability of Extraction

The concept of 'extractive-ness' exists on a spectrum, rather than as a binary state. Systems can be mildly or severely extractive in impact. They can be partially or solely extractive in their operations. Furthermore, extraction isn't always constant; a system may exhibit periods of intense extraction interspersed with periods of less or no extraction. This means a system can be partially extractive at certain times or under specific conditions, even if it isn't always fully extractive.

The tipping point where extraction becomes apparent often lies in a convergence of objective indicators and subjective experience, signaling when the extractiveness becomes undeniable.

Additionally, extraction can operate cumulatively across multiple systems or over time. Individuals rarely experience extraction from a single source in isolation—they may simultaneously experience extraction in workplace dynamics, economic constraints, and interpersonal relationships. These layered extractions may compound, creating cumulative psychic and physical toll that can make even minor extractive encounters feel disproportionately overwhelming. What might appear as a mild extraction in isolation can become the critical threshold when layered atop existing extractive pressures, explaining why seemingly small extractions can provoke unexpectedly intense responses.

Vantage Point: Internal vs. External Analysis; Historical vs. Contemporary

An observer's vantage point shapes the assessment of a system's extractiveness. This is largely determined by whether the observer is inside or outside of the system and, if inside the system, their position within its hierarchy. Inside a system, one can be both extracted from and an extractor of others.

Internal Analysis: Subjective Perception

When analyzing a system from within, particularly from the perspective of an individual participant, the assessment relies heavily on subjective perception and 'feeling-toned' experience. This aligns with a Jungian analysis, where the 'extractive-ness' is arbitrated by the individual's Self.

Key questions

- Do individuals feel that the system or relationship is extractive—and if so, to what degree? Is it partially extractive, making some aspects or periods feel exploitative?

- How does this perceived extractiveness impact their sense of well-being, autonomy, or personal growth? Are these impacts felt consistently, or only under certain extractive conditions?

Crucially, an individual's position within the system's hierarchy profoundly shapes this perception. Those at the bottom, from whom value is primarily extracted, are far more likely to perceive the system as extractive. They are experiencing its negative impacts directly, even if the system is only partially or occasionally extractive. Conversely, those closer to the top, who disproportionately benefit from the concentrated value, may perceive the system as equitable, beneficial, or even not extractive at all, as their experience is one of net gain, potentially overlooking the partial or occasional extractiveness experienced by others.

Subjective analysis is particularly effective for contemporary observation—due to the near over-availability of opinions and reactions from members within extractive systems.

External/Historical Analysis

When analyzing a system from the outside - either through vantage point historically, the inquiry shifts towards more objective and empirical observations, aligning with a Marxian perspective. Here, the focus is on identifying structural patterns and outcomes, which can reveal patterns of partial extraction.

Primary questions include

- Is there a discernible class hierarchy or stratification within the system that facilitates extraction, even if it's not universally applied or consistently severe?

- Is there an evident concentration of surplus value, resources, or benefits flowing disproportionately upward through that hierarchy, or from the system's periphery to its core, suggesting partial extractiveness in its design or operation?

- What do historical or contemporary data (economic, social, environmental) say about how the system was perceived as extractive by the collective writ large? Do these perceptions indicate consistent extractiveness, or more localized/periodic extraction?

- Was the system extractive to the collective overall, in aggregate, considering its total impact, or were only specific segments or periods subject to extraction?

- What are the observable patterns of extraction, and what was the quantifiable amount being extracted? Does the evidence suggest continuous extraction or only partial, episodic extraction?

- Was the extraction voluntary, suggested, or enforced, either through sociocultural apparatus or through overt force, even if limited in scope or duration?

Applying the Framework

This framework effectively analyzes all scales of human interaction—from examining entire civilizations and macrosystems down to assessing a single exchange with one's manager. The core principles remain consistent regardless of scope.

In praxis, this comprehensive framework first seeks evidence of extractive patterns in the relationship between the individual and the system (subjective perception), and secondarily, assesses the degree and variability of the extractiveness. In contemporary contexts, the subjective 'feeling-tone' of individuals offers critical insight into the lived experience of extraction. For external or historical analyses, objective evidence of hierarchical value concentration provides the structural and empirical basis for judgment, helping to identify the scope and nature of partial extractiveness.

The degrees and amounts of extractiveness are highly variable. In contemporary analysis, the critical juncture—or—tipping point—where extraction becomes undeniably apparent often lies in the subjective perception of the system by the individuals within it—particularly those from whom value is being siphoned—even when the system's extractiveness is not total but rather partial, episodic, or localized. This is often confirmed by objective measures revealing structural imbalances. The interplay between individual experience (Jungian) and systemic structure (Marxian) is essential for a complete understanding, especially when analyzing extractive systems through a modern lens.

Intent

This framework proposes a way to understand extractive systems: by systematically articulating the patterns of extraction that operate within them, distinct from their material structures. It is a framework for thinking and feeling, not a calculator for measuring. It's designed to help perceive the human and psychological impacts of systems, not just their functional aspects. Inspired by Jungian thought, this approach provides a subjective yet practical lens for understanding the systems we participate in.

By examining historical examples across five millennia, we can trace the consistent 'blueprint of extraction,' revealing how the collective shadow manifests and engages the individual shadow. In contemporary terms, this framework empowers us to inquire into and analyze the impact of participating in extractive systems, whether it's our engagement with social media or our day-to-day interactions with colleagues and superiors.

Rationale for the Framework

Jung's structure of the Psyche has been profoundly valuable to me during my personal journey—it provided a scaffolding system for inquiry. My framework has been the methodological way to see and articulate patterns of extraction. When an symbol would be activated in my unconscious through active imagining, this framework helped to understand the symbol more deeply; to see the telic movement of the activated symbol. It also helped to analyze the archetypal symbols from historical contexts from the collective unconscious that resonated with my own psyche. Through repeated use its proven to be valuable for not only examining symbols that have emerged from active imaging, but for examining the underlying psychic material of mundane patterns in everyday life —especially when the charge around a situation felt disproportionate to the event.

The Architecture, The Model, & The Facets

In my vocation, I've been a systems thinker for the better part of three decades —in the field of experience architecture and digital design. I think in systems and the impact of a given system on the humans within it. That impact upon the human user is assessed through qualitative and quantitative research. That blend of thinking led to this framework.

My conceptual framework offers a methodical lens for observing and analyzing extractive systems—as they have been designed or have evolved to be —through three core interrelated components: the **Architecture**, the **Model**, and the **Facets**. I define the **Architecture** using three terms: *Extractive System*, *Paraextractive System*, and *Subextractive System*. These terms represent levels of hierarchy and complex relationships within the macrosystem.

The **Architecture** functions through the **Model.** That **Model** is how the **Architecture** manifests or functions within a civilization system or culture.

Beyond the architecture and model, this framework also includes **Facets**. Within a civilization, they are the sociocultural apparatus of the **Architecture** and its manifestation through the **Model**. These **Facets** serve as analytical lenses, providing a way to observe how the **Architecture** expresses the **Model** socioculturally through integrated belief systems across different civilizations and historical periods, from the Bronze Age through our current age. While the **Facets** are neutral, they can nonetheless enable extraction through embedded belief systems, cultural trends, or social enforcement systems. They may operate independently or in concert, and their hierarchies are often dynamic, with one **Facet** potentially holding authoritative sway over another depending on the era. The **Facets**, since they represent sociocultural apparatus, enable a way to integrate Jungian concepts *into* the overall system rather than overlay them *onto* the system.

How the Architecture, the Model, and the Facets come together

Essentially, the relationship between the **Architecture** + the **Model** is the extractive (or Paraextractive or Subextractive) system—the relationship between the **Model** + the Individual is how the extractive system acts upon Individuals. The **Facets** provide the sociocultural apparatus of a given environment and are used system-wide. The relationship between the **Architecture** + the **Model** is primarily influenced by Marx—but not exclusively Marxian—Jung's 'collective' psychic aspects of the system express here as well through the **Facets**. The **Model** + the Individual are a synthesis of Marxian and Jungian concepts—here the 'individual' psyche parts interact with their 'collective' counterparts. Through a syntonic relationship between the 'collective' aspects and the 'individual' parts of the psyche—individuals are influenced by or embody the psychic energy of the **Architecture**.

Examining the **Facets** across the **Architecture** and the **Model** show us the sociocultural apparatus used by the **Architecture** to act upon the Individual within the **Model**. When looking at the Individual within the **Model** using the **Facets,** we see the sociocultural apparatus from the perspective of an individual within the extractive system.

The Architecture

Extractive systems - systems that consume more from the collective than they supply to the collective. Systems that, either by conscious design or unconscious evolution, asymmetrically extract something (e.g., a resource, attention, money, credibility, engagement) from the humans existing within the system without adequately compensating them for the exchange - concentrating the aggregate value toward the top of the collective. This level of the system is the 'host' or 'macro' extractive system.

Examples

- **E-commerce platforms** - Extract listing fees, transaction fees, advertising costs, and data from sellers in exchange for marketplace access.

- **Feudalism** - Extracted labor, agricultural output (e.g., crops, livestock), and military service from serfs and peasants in exchange for protection and access to land which was ultimately owned by the lord.

- **Social media platforms** - Extract attention, personal data, and data from behavioral patterns in exchange for deceptively 'free' social connection.

Paraextractive systems - systems that operate autonomously or semi-autonomously within a host/macro extractive system. They may also function parallel to or in conjunction with paraextractive systems within the host/macro extractive system. They extract something directly or indirectly from the collective within the system beyond what is extracted by the host/macro extractive system.

Examples

- **Third-party services within dominant platforms** - These operate semi-autonomously, often invisibly, within major e-commerce ecosystems, extracting additional value through premium placement, specialized advertising tools, or markup on logistics services.

- **Company Stores** (within Early Industrial Factories/Mining Operations) extracted (through a relationship with the company owner) a portion of workers' already suppressed wages through inflated prices for essential goods, creating debt bondage and limiting economic independence.

- **Predatory lending operations in underserved areas** - Operate within the broader context of financial systems, but add their own extraction through high-interest short-term loans.

Subextractive systems - systems that extract on behalf of, or in addition to, a host/macro extractive system or paraextractive system. They are dependent on a host/macro system or paraextractive system and typically represent the level where the direct enforcement of the higher-level systems occurs, often having direct access to the humans within the system.

Examples

- **Product fulfillment services** - Completely dependent on major e-commerce platforms, these systems extract additional fees from sellers for storage, packaging, and shipping on behalf of the platform.

- **Corvée Labor Overseers** (within Bronze Age Despotic Kingdoms; their host extractive system) - Extracted forced labor and additional demands for resources or time from the populace on behalf of the king or ruling elite, ensuring the completion of monumental projects or agricultural quotas.

- **Credit reporting agencies serving financial institutions** - Extract personal financial data from consumers to serve lenders' risk assessment goals. They're dependent on the financial system and exist primarily to enhance lenders' ability to extract value through the perception of more precise risk pricing.

The Model

Hierarchy: Asymmetrical levels, roles, or groups within a system that is inherently based on an imbalance of power or control. These roles, groups, or levels may be dynamic (*final; teleological*) or legacy (*causal; historic*). This hierarchy may be materially or psychically imposed, explicit or implied - and may or may not offer potential methods to negotiate or express agency.

Examples

- king > serf
- CEO > admin assistant
- director > actor
- senator > page

- agent > artist
- banker > loan applicant
- influencer > follower
- professor > student

Subject: The role or group that is recipient of the extraction - where the resource is being directed to.

Examples

- king
- chief
- boss

- culture
- president
- administrator

Object: The role or group that is being extracted from - the where is the resource coming from.

Examples

- citizens
- users
- employees

- everyone below my level
- followers
- subordinates

Resource: Something of perceived value - the thing that's being extracted.

Examples

- emojis
- trees
- cattle
- credibility
- humans
- ideas
- attention
- money
- time
- your pics and your data

Method: How the resource is being extracted - the processes, belief systems, technologies, and/or practices.

Examples

- colonization
- market domination/ monopolization
- work ethics
- inflammatory rhetoric
- membership/sense of belonging
- internship

Reason/Purpose: The underlying motivation, goal, or ideological justification for the extraction.

Examples

- expansion
- sustaining growth
- fear of losing corporate healthcare
- value increase
- manifest destiny doctrine
- civilizing indigenous populations
- because everyone else is doing it
- because that's how its always been done

Impacts/Consequences: The overall holistic effects of the extraction on the extracted-from.

Examples

- loss of tribal territories
- vanishing rainforest
- compromising dignity

- embarrassment
- loss of privacy
- burnout

Resistance/Contestation: The forms of opposition or struggle against the extractive system.

Examples

- expression of personal boundaries
- protest
- abandonment of brand
- public expression

- reclamation
- breaking up with a narcissist
- suing for overtime
- unsubscribing from an app's texts

The Facets

Governance & Power - Politics, global impacts, and the structures of control

- **Structures**: Empires, states, monarchies, legislative bodies, international organizations, penal institutions, military power

- **Enables extraction through**: Taxation, tribute, conscription, bureaucracies, legal/penal frameworks, political dominance, imposition of policies, enforcement and incarceration

Economy & Labor - Work, financial, and the broad production/distribution of resources

- **Structures**: Agriculture, trade networks, currency systems, industrial production, wage labor, financial markets, global supply chains

- **Enables extraction through**: Slavery, serfdom, wage suppression, debt, unequal trade, market manipulation, resource appropriation, financial speculation, corporate loyalty

Culture - Shared societal norms, values, arts, media, and popular practices, distinct from explicit belief systems

- **Structures**: Artistic expression, oral traditions, written media, entertainment (secular forms), fashion, social trends, popular narratives

- **Enables extraction through**: Control of narratives, cultural appropriation, commodification of cultural forms, attention harvesting (in secular media/ entertainment), shaping consumer behavior, hustle culture

Religion & Spirituality - Organized belief systems, spiritual practices, and their institutions

- **Structures**: Religious institutions, theological doctrines, spiritual rituals, sacred sites, personal spiritual practices

- **Enables extraction through**: Tithes/donations, spiritual labor, control over beliefs/conscience, commodification of spiritual experiences/healing, ideological conformity, suppression of alternative spiritualities

Knowledge & Learning Systems - Creation, dissemination, and control of information, education, and understanding

- **Structures**: Oral traditions, scribal cultures, academies, universities, scientific methods, public education, digital learning platforms, data analytics, intellectual property

- **Enables extraction through**: Control of information, censorship, intellectual property rights, educational stratification, commodification of knowledge, shaping narratives, institutional gatekeeping

Tools & Technology - Physical and systemic apparatus and innovations used for various purposes, from creation to extraction

- **Structures**: Agricultural tools, weaponry, printing press, industrial machinery, communication networks, computing hardware, AI algorithms, digital platforms themselves (as tools—although they can also be an extractive, paraextractive, or subextractive system on their own)

- **Enables extraction through**: Control of production means, leveraging technological advantage, planned obsolescence, designed-in extractive features, barriers to access

Personal & Inner Life - The individual human experience, self, and immediate family/household

- **Structures**: Individual well-being, psychological state, personal development, family structures, identity

- **Enables extraction through**: Psychological manipulation, commodification of identity, erosion of mental/emotional health, atomization, loss of individual agency, exploitation of family labor

Community & Relationships - Social bonds beyond the immediate family; the broader social fabric

- **Structures**: Social networks, community organizations, civic life, collective action, social capital

- **Enables extraction through**: Erosion of social trust, fragmentation of communities, exploitation of social capital, breakdown of solidarity, divisive social engineering

Shelter & Place - The fundamental human connection to physical space, home, and environment

- **Structures**: Housing, land, environment, natural resources, sacred sites, physical territories

- **Enables extraction through**: Displacement, gentrification, land appropriation, environmental degradation, resource depletion, destruction of cultural heritage tied to place, loss of 'Genius Loci'

Distinct 'Military' and 'Penal' facets have been intentionally omitted as discrete facets from this list because my framework focuses on the sociocultural apparatus of civilian life. While not separate facets, their functions are represented within the **'Governance & Power'** facet, where they serve as enforcement mechanisms of governing bodies—the military targeting perceived external threats and penal systems focusing on presumed internal threats. For a more comprehensive analysis of a civilization's sociocultural apparatus, encompassing its entire civilian, penal, and military functions, these would be included as distinct facets.

A Brief History of Extraction— Revisited

An idea is weighed through its use. We'll use the Architecture, the Model, and the Facets on two examples as case studies.

Having provided many historical examples of extraction, ranging from 'Just Last Week' back through five millennia to the Bronze Age, and introduced the analytic framework of Architecture, Model, and Facets, we can now begin to see patterns by applying this framework to those examples. This synthesized Jungian (interior; subjective) and Marxian (exterior; material) analytical lens reveals the interconnections between the outer mechanics and the internal psychic impact of extraction.

At this juncture, you may be asking yourself why this level of analysis is relevant in a framework that professes to have roots in Jung's concepts. Jung taught me to seek vectors where the collective shadow (and related archetype, collective complex, or collective neurosis) intersects or apprehends the individual shadow (or the broader psyche, individual complex, or individual neurosis) through their congruent relationship. I created this framework to serve that endeavor methodically. This approach enables observation of the layers of extraction to account for the cumulative impact of any and all layers above the immediate layer. The goal is not absolute historical sociocultural accuracy, but rather, a subjective, qualitative examination of the prominent archetypes and telic movement within the symbol of 'the system'—to understand why the symbol of 'feudal system' functions as a psychologically charged archetypal pattern that continues to resonate in the collective unconscious and express through our own unconscious material.

First, we'll use the Architecture, the Model, and the Facets for the eras to see the emergence of the sociocultural apparatus and the layers of extraction. Let's explore Feudalism & Guild structures:

Case Study One: The Medieval Era (500-1500 CE)

Our previous example

Feudalism institutionalized extraction through land ownership. Peasants provided labor and tribute to lords in exchange for 'protection.' Urban guilds emerged as a secondary nearly-equal system, only nominally deferring to the lords. Guilds controlled craft production and trade while providing mutual protection for artisans and merchants. Though guilds operated with autonomy in cities, they remained subject to feudal lords through taxation and charters.

Over time, powerful guild cities accumulated enough wealth to challenge traditional feudal authority, creating tensions between urban commercial power and rural landed nobility—resulting in various level of deference to the feudal system.

Human roles

- You're a peasant, bound to the land you work. Your lord provides a small plot for your family and theoretical protection, but you owe him days of labor on his fields (corvée), a portion of your harvest, and fees for using his mill or oven. You feel stuck; leaving means starvation or becoming a bandit.

- You're a young apprentice in a bustling medieval guild. You dedicate years to learning your craft, working long hours for little pay, often living with your master. You gain skills, but your labor directly enriches the master, and the guild controls your path to becoming independent, demanding loyalty and adherence to its strict rules.

- You're a minor noble, loyal to a powerful duke. The duke demands your military service, your knights, and a portion of the taxes you collect from your own meager lands whenever he rides to war or needs funds. You comply, knowing your own status and security depend entirely on his continued favor and protection.

First, we'll apply the Architecture, the Model, and the Facets to analyze the era's civilization itself.

Medieval Feudalism & Guild Era (500-1500 CE)

The Civilization

Medieval society operated as a vast psychosocial apparatus where multiple overlapping systems drew wealth, labor, and loyalty upward through rigid hierarchies, creating archetypal patterns of domination and submission that still resonate in the collective unconscious. At its heart lay feudalism—operating through manorialism to control land and the people bound to it—supported by nearly equal guilds that monopolized urban crafts and trade.

These systems created not just economic extraction but profound psychological conditioning, embedding archetypal patterns of authority, obedience, and hierarchical identity that shaped the medieval psyche and continue to influence collective shadow material around power, servitude, and social position.

Architecture: Level One - Macro/Host Level

The layers of the system. In this case this is the top level—the host or macro system. Feudalism and Guilds were the two primary systems operating at this level.

Extractive System: Feudalism and Guilds

The two prominent systems in this era were Feudalism (Operating Through Manorialism) and guilds. Guilds were only nominally deferential to lords, and nearly rivaled their power - in this case study, we'll examine both.

Model

The mechanics; how the system acts upon its members. Here, we have two to consider—Feudalism and Guilds.

Hierarchy

- **Feudalism** (operating through manorialism): Kings at apex (often nominal), powerful Lords as direct territorial rulers through manorial control, knights/vassals bound by personal oaths, peasants (free, villein, serf) bound to the land in ascending degrees of subjugation

- **Guilds**: Master craftsmen dominating journeymen and apprentices in rigid advancement hierarchies

Subjects

- **Feudalism** (operating through manorialism): Kings and Lords

- **Guilds**: Guild Masters

Objects

- **Feudalism** (through manorialism): Peasants and anyone below the extractors' class or level

- **Guilds**: Anyone below the Guild Master

Resources

- **Feudalism** (through manorialism): Agricultural surplus, corvée labor, military service, rents, fees, absolute loyalty, embodied submission

- **Guilds**: Market monopolization, craft knowledge hoarding, years of unpaid/underpaid labor extraction

Methods

- **Feudalism** (through manorialism): Personal oaths binding souls to hierarchy, land tenure systems creating hereditary bondage, manorial courts enforcing psychological submission, military retinues projecting dominance

- **Guilds**: Apprenticeship systems extracting labor while conditioning obedience, monopoly controls eliminating alternatives

Reason/Purpose

- **Feudalism** (through manorialism): Maintain hierarchical social order that concentrates wealth and power while psychologically conditioning acceptance of fixed social position

- **Guilds**: Control urban production while creating rigid advancement hierarchies that channel ambition into servitude

Impacts/Consequences

- **Feudalism** (through manorialism): Feudal lords owned not just land but the very identity of those bound to it—peasants internalized their subordinate position as natural and divinely ordained, creating deep archetypal patterns of authority and submission

- **Guilds**: Guild masters controlled apprentices' entire social identity, extracting years of labor while conditioning psychological acceptance of hierarchical advancement through prolonged servitude

Resistance/Contestation

- **Feudalism** (through manorialism): Peasant revolts (Jacquerie, Wat Tyler's Rebellion) representing shadow eruptions against internalized oppression, serf flight to towns as escape from archetypal imprisonment, passive resistance through work slowdowns and sabotage

- **Guilds**: Journeymen guild revolts challenging master dominance, underground networks resisting monopoly control

Facets

This is the psychological-material, the sociocultural apparatus that operates through archetypal conditioning across all life domains. Medieval civilization was highly and obviously stratified; mobility was limited and a person generally remained at the level at which they were born.

- **Governance & Power**: Feudal oaths binding individual identity to hierarchical position; guild charters creating professional caste systems

- **Economy & Labor**: Corvée labor and guild monopolies transforming human energy into elite wealth while conditioning acceptance of exploitation

- **Culture**: Divine hierarchy mythology normalizing fixed social order as cosmic truth, creating archetypal patterns of ruler/ruled

- **Religion & Spirituality**: The Church sanctified feudal bondage as God's will, embedding spiritual authority behind material extraction

- **Knowledge & Learning**: Lords restricting peasant education to maintain ignorance; Guild masters hoarding craft secrets to preserve dominance hierarchies

- **Tools & Technology**: Feudal lords monopolizing land-working implements; guild masters controlling workshop access, creating technological dependency

- **Personal & Inner Life**: Feudalism conditioning deep psychological obedience and acceptance of 'natural' inferiority; guilds channeling personal ambition through hierarchical servitude

- **Community & Relationships**: Manorial courts structuring social bonds around hierarchical deference; guild networks creating professional identity through submission to masters

- **Shelter & Place**: Feudal land control creating psychological bondage to place; guild housing systems binding workers to master dependency

Architecture: Level Two - Paraextractive Systems

This is the second level of the system architecture. These systems operate autonomously or semi-autonomously within the host/macro extractive system.

Feudal lords ruled through manorial extraction and guilds ruled the urban workspace. Other institutions, like The Church, carved out their own psychological-material territories, creating multiple simultaneous channels of submission and upward resource flow. These systems were both extractor to those below, yet they were extractees to the levels above. They usually extracted on behalf of the level(s) further up, and add to it for their own benefit.

In Medieval civilization there were several paraextractive systems. Each exerted its own particular influence through the facets.

Paraextractive System: The Church - Spiritual-Economic Empire

Model

- **Hierarchy**: Pope as divine representative, cardinals, archbishops, bishops, priests creating complete spiritual authority chain with temporal power

- **Subjects**: Pope, cardinals, archbishops, bishops

- **Objects**: Congregants. Those in need of an 'official' sanction from the Church. Anyone further down the hierarchy

- **Resources**: Tithes (10% of all income), sacrament fees for every life transition, vast landholdings, monastic labor, absolute spiritual adherence, guilt-driven donations

- **Methods**: Mandatory confession creating psychological control, sacrament monopoly ensuring dependency, canon law operating parallel court systems, monastic communities channeling spiritual energy into Church wealth

- **Reason/Purpose**: Extract wealth through spiritual monopoly while conditioning psychological submission to divine hierarchy embodied in Church authority

- **Impacts/Consequences**: The Church created total psychological dependency by controlling access to salvation; every major life event required payment, creating archetypal patterns of spiritual authority and guilt-driven compliance that extracted both material wealth and psychic energy

- **Resistance/Contestation**: Heretical movements (Cathars, Lollards) representing shadow eruptions against spiritual exploitation, anti-clerical sentiment challenging Church psychological dominance

Facets

- **Religion & Spirituality**: The Church provided absolute authority for material extraction through salvation monopoly, ordaining the laws of the feudal lord as divinely sanctioned

- **Personal & Inner Life**: The Church dominated through confession and guilt conditioning, creating archetypal patterns of spiritual submission that served material ends

Paraextractive System: Guild Masters - Craft Controllers

Model

- **Hierarchy**: Master craftsmen dominating apprentice/journeymen hierarchies while maintaining guild solidarity against outside threats

- **Subjects**: Guild Masters

- **Objects**: Apprentice/Journeymen and other subordinates

- **Resources**: Years of unpaid/underpaid labor extraction, entrance fees, workshop control, craft knowledge monopolization

- **Methods**: Total life control over apprentices, advancement gate-keeping, psychological conditioning through craft identity

- **Reason/Purpose**: Extract maximum labor value while conditioning psychological acceptance of craft hierarchy and urban social order

- **Impacts/Consequences**: Guild masters created total psychological dependency by controlling not just work but housing, social relationships, and professional identity of subordinates, establishing archetypal patterns of craft mastery and professional submission

- **Resistance/Contestation**: Journeymen fraternities, apprentice flight, underground craft networks challenging guild monopolies

Facets

- **Economy & Labor**: Wealth accumulation through multi-layered labor extraction and craft knowledge monopolization

- **Personal & Inner Life**: Identity reinforced through patriarchal craft authority and psychological dominance over subordinates' entire life trajectories

Paraextractive System: Royal Bureaucracies - Centralizing Tax Systems

Model

- **Hierarchy**: Royal officials (chancellors, exchequer officers) bypassing feudal lords to create direct Crown authority over citizens

- **Subjects**: Royal officials

- **Objects**: Citizens of every level

- **Resources**: Direct taxes (hearth tax, scutage), tolls, customs duties, judicial fees, fines, loyalty transferred from local to central authority

- **Methods**: Professional administration, written records, royal courts, common law development, standing officials creating impersonal authority structures

- **Reason/Purpose**: Centralize extraction by bypassing local lords, creating direct subject-Crown relationships that channel wealth and psychological allegiance upward

- **Impacts/Consequences**: Royal bureaucracies slowly dissolved personal feudal bonds, replacing them with impersonal state authority that created new archetypal patterns of subject-sovereign relationships, conditioning acceptance of abstract institutional power

- **Resistance/Contestation**: Baronial revolts (Magna Carta) representing elite resistance to centralization, peasant resistance to new royal taxes

Facets

- **Governance & Power**: Royal Bureaucracies institutionalized impersonal authority, replacing personal bonds

- **Personal & Inner Life:** Subjects adapted to abstract state power of Royal Bureaucracies, creating archetypal patterns of citizenship-submission

Paraextractive System: Moneylenders - Financial Networks

Model

- **Hierarchy**: Wealthy lending families/individuals creating financial dependency networks across social classes

- **Subjects**: Moneylenders

- **Objects**: People in need of financial assistance

- **Resources**: Interest payments, principal repayment, collateral seizure, debt bondage service, psychological anxiety around financial obligation

- **Methods**: Interest loans, collateral leverage, debt contract enforcement, exploiting capital scarcity and Christian usury prohibitions

- **Reason/Purpose**: Accumulate wealth through financial dependency while creating psychological patterns of debt anxiety and creditor deference

- **Impacts/Consequences**: Moneylenders (often marginalized communities) created financial extraction networks that generated wealth through others' necessity, establishing archetypal patterns of debtor anxiety and creditor power that transcended traditional social hierarchies

- **Resistance/Contestation**: Debt defaults, popular resentment manifesting as anti-Semitic violence, royal expulsion decrees representing projection of debt shadow onto vulnerable communities

Facets

- **Economy & Labor**: Christian usury prohibitions created financial extraction niches

- **Personal & Inner Life**: Permeated by debt anxiety and creditor psychological dominance

Paraextractive System: Free Companies - Violence for Hire

Model

- **Hierarchy**: Military captains commanding fighting forces, authority derived from violence capacity and contract negotiation

- **Subjects**: Mercenaries, free military captains

- **Objects**: Local communities, towns, and individuals who were subject to plunder, ransom, or who pay for protection

- **Resources**: Military pay, plunder, ransom, protection money, psychological dominance through fear

- **Methods**: Direct violence, intimidation, military contracting, operating outside traditional authority structures

- **Reason/Purpose**: Extract wealth through violence monopolization and fear conditioning, creating archetypal patterns of predator-prey relationships

- **Impacts/Consequences**: Mercenary companies commodified violence, extracting payment through military services while conditioning psychological submission through fear, creating archetypal patterns around violence, protection, and survival anxiety

- **Resistance/Contestation**: Local militias, fortified towns, appeals to feudal lords for protection against mercenary predation

Facets

- **Governance & Power**: Free Companies operated through raw violence capacity outside traditional hierarchies

- **Personal & Inner Life**: Medieval survival conditions shaped humans through fear and dependency on protection

Architecture: Level Three - Subextractive Systems

This layer embodies the active enforcement mechanisms of the layers above. The First and Second Layers demanded intermediaries wielding hierarchical authority to actualize their imperatives. These intermediaries orchestrated routine extraction.

Subextractive System: Manorial Bailiffs - Lords' Direct Agents

Model

- **Hierarchy**: Bailiff/steward as lord's psychological representative, positioned above peasants but below lords, embodying hierarchical submission-dominance

- **Subjects**: Bailiffs

- **Objects**: Village Reeves, Peasants

- **Resources**: Supervisory authority, modest privileges, psychological investment in maintaining hierarchy

- **Methods**: Daily labor surveillance, rent collection, manorial court administration, psychological conditioning of peasant compliance

- **Reason/Purpose**: Implement feudal extraction while psychologically identifying with lord's interests, creating middle-management archetypal patterns

- **Impacts/Consequences**: Bailiffs internalized hierarchical authority, becoming psychological enforcers who maintained extraction systems by embodying both submission (to lords) and dominance (over peasants), creating archetypal patterns of middle-management identification with elite interests

- **Resistance/Contestation**: Peasant resentment toward bailiffs as class traitors, bailiff anxiety about position between conflicting loyalties

Facets

- **Personal & Inner Life**: Identity fractured between submission to lords and dominance over peasants, creating psychological investment in hierarchical legitimacy through middle-management authority

- **Governance & Power**: Administrative control exercised through internalized lordly authority, implementing extraction while psychologically identifying with elite interests against peasant communities

Subextractive System: Village Reeves - Peasant Self-Enforcers

Model

- **Hierarchy**: Village reeve as peasant-turned-overseer, positioned above fellow villagers but below bailiffs/lords, embodying peer-enforcement dynamics

- **Subjects**: Reeves

- **Objects**: Fellow peasants and villagers

- **Resources**: Limited supervisory authority over neighbors, modest exemptions from fees, psychological elevation above peasant peers

- **Methods**: Labor organization for demesne work, rent collection from community members, village dispute mediation, peer surveillance and compliance enforcement

- **Reason/Purpose**: Implement manorial extraction through peasant self-policing while creating archetypal patterns of community betrayal and horizontal oppression

- **Impacts/Consequences**: Reeves internalized the psychology of collaborative enforcement, becoming peasant agents who maintained extraction by policing their own communities, creating archetypal patterns of peer surveillance and the 'elevated collaborator' who gains modest privilege through betraying class solidarity

- **Resistance/Contestation**: Village ostracism of reeves, community pressure to resist lord's demands, reeve torn between village loyalty and manorial duty

Facets

- **Personal & Inner Life**: Split between community belonging and collaborative enforcement, creating psychological isolation within one's own class

- **Community & Relationships**: Social bonds strained through peer surveillance and enforcement responsibilities, normalizing horizontal oppression within peasant communities

Subextractive System: Journeymen - Intermediaries of the Guild Master

Model

- **Hierarchy**: Journeymen exploiting apprentices while simultaneously being dominated by guild masters, creating psychological investment in hierarchical advancement

- **Subjects**: Journeymen

- **Objects**: Apprentices and junior craftsmen under their supervision

- **Resources**: Apprentice labor extraction, supervision fees, workshop authority over beginners, selective craft knowledge transmission

- **Methods**: Disciplinary control over apprentices, advancement conditioning, psychological modeling of 'earned authority' through craft competence

- **Reason/Purpose**: Extract labor value from subordinates while demonstrating worthiness for eventual mastership, reinforcing craft hierarchy through middle-management psychology

- **Impacts/Consequences**: Journeymen internalized dual extraction dynamics—exploiting those below while accepting exploitation from above—creating powerful psychological investment in maintaining the guild system and archetypal patterns of 'deserved' hierarchical advancement

- **Resistance/Contestation**: Journeymen fraternities organizing against masters, collective bargaining for advancement timelines, underground networks bypassing guild restrictions

Facets

- **Economy & Labor**: Identity structured around proving worthiness for advancement through effective subordinate management

- **Personal & Inner Life**: Psychological conditioning balanced submission to authority with exercise of power over others, creating complex investment in hierarchical legitimacy

Subextractive System: Local Priests - Church Agents

Model

- **Hierarchy**: Parish priest as immediate spiritual authority, representing Church hierarchy while living among parishioners

- **Subjects**: Parish priests

- **Objects**: Parishioners

- **Resources**: Tithe collection, sacrament fees, moral authority, confession-based psychological control

- **Methods**: Sermon delivery, confession administration, community moral surveillance, guilt conditioning

- **Reason/Purpose**: Implement Church extraction at local level while maintaining spiritual authority that legitimizes material demands

- **Impacts/Consequences**: Parish priests created intimate psychological control through confession and moral authority, extracting wealth while conditioning guilt, obedience, and spiritual dependency at the community level

- **Resistance/Contestation**: Folk religious practices, complaints about clerical fees and behavior, resistance to Church moral control

Facets

- **Religion & Spirituality** and **Personal & Inner Life**: Inner life was compromised through confession, guilt conditioning, and constant spiritual surveillance, making private thoughts subject to ecclesiastical control

- **Community & Relationships**: Social bonds were structured around spiritual hierarchy and moral policing, with relationships mediated through church authority and religious conformity requirements

Subextractive System: Millers/Bakers: Monopoly Holders

Model

- **Hierarchy**: Service providers holding local monopolies, positioned between lords (who grant monopolies) and peasants (who require services)

- **Subjects**: Millers, bakers

- **Objects**: Peasants

- **Resources**: Mandatory service fees (banalities), often significantly above competitive prices

- **Methods**: Monopoly enforcement, service dependency, leveraging lack of alternatives

- **Reason/Purpose**: Generate additional extraction revenue for lords while creating local dependency relationships

- **Impacts/Consequences**: Millers and bakers embodied economic dependency by controlling essential services, creating archetypal patterns of monopoly power and consumer helplessness in daily life necessities

- **Resistance/Contestation**: Illegal home processing, complaints to lords, community resentment toward monopoly holders

Facets

- **Economy & Labor**: Daily survival dependency was engineered through essential food processing monopolies, making economic relationships inescapable extraction cycles

- **Personal & Inner Life**: Psychological adaptation to routine exploitation through vital service control, normalizing extraction as the price of basic sustenance

The Psychological Reality

This system created not just economic extraction but profound archetypal conditioning where people internalized hierarchical positions as natural, divine, and personally meaningful. The multiple overlapping hierarchies ensured that nearly everyone experienced both submission and domination, creating complex psychological investments in maintaining the system even while being exploited by it. These archetypal patterns—the obedient serf, the loyal vassal, the aspiring apprentice, the dutiful parishioner—became internalized identity structures that made resistance psychologically difficult even when materially beneficial.

Shadow Dynamics and Resistance

People contested these systems through shadow eruptions—peasant revolts that temporarily inverted hierarchies, heretical movements that challenged spiritual authority, urban uprisings that attacked symbols of domination. But the system's psychological depth made it remarkably adaptive. Resistance was often contained and channeled into approved forms (pilgrimage, monastery life, approved guild advancement) or was projected onto scapegoats (Cathars, Jews, Moors, heretics, witches) rather than challenging the fundamental archetypal structures.

The Archetypal Legacy

Medieval extraction worked through psychological subjugation—making people complicit in their own exploitation by embedding hierarchical identity so deeply that submission felt like natural social order. The concentration of land, tools, and knowledge in elite hands was maintained not just by force but by archetypal patterns that made hierarchy feel inevitable, meaningful, and even spiritually significant.

This created archetypal residues that persist in the collective unconscious: the loyal employee, the dutiful citizen, the aspiring professional, the faithful believer—all containing shadow elements of the medieval serf, vassal, apprentice, and parishioner. These patterns continue to facilitate contemporary extraction by making hierarchical submission feel psychologically natural rather than historically constructed.

The pattern reveals how effective extraction systems permeate not just external resources but internal psychological structures, creating archetypal investments in hierarchy that make people participants in their own exploitation —a dynamic that transcends all historical periods and continues to shape collective shadow material around power, authority, and social position.

Civilization as Container

That is a look at the multi-layered architecture of Feudalism and Guilds. Despite its overall decentralization, it imposed rigid, localized control over labor and resources. The host system was intricately complemented by 'Paraextractive' entities—like the Church, royal bureaucracies, guild masters, independent moneylenders, and free company mercenary bands—each emerged as powerful, often nearly autonomous, centers of extraction, frequently exploiting existing societal needs or prohibitions to generate their own wealth and influence. Finally, 'Subextractive' agents (e.g., bailiffs, reeves, local priests, millers/bakers) acted as direct implementers, ensuring the flow of resources at the most granular level.

Across all these architectural layers, the 'Facets' highlight persistent patterns in how extraction was achieved. There's a consistent concentration of control and power—whether through land tenure, guild rules, spiritual authority, or monopoly over essential services—always directed towards benefiting the extractor.

This control was deeply embedded and legitimized by sociocultural norms, with culture and religion playing crucial roles in normalizing hierarchies, enforcing obedience, and validating the demands of the powerful. The exploitation of labor and economic opportunity is a fundamental thread, structuring all relationships to ensure that value generated by the majority flowed upwards. Furthermore, control over knowledge and essential tools consistently limited agency and reinforced established extractive structures. These patterns reveal that medieval extraction was not merely a top-down command, but a complex, pervasive system woven into the very fabric of society, leveraging every aspect from daily routines and community structures to deeply held beliefs to concentrate wealth and power.

Through this analysis of the civilization we've seen the container for all of the collective sociocultural elements and power structures. The system that houses—the archetypes, the collective consciousness, the collective unconscious, the collective shadow, the collective neurosis. It maps the landscape that the psyche engages with.

The Humans in the Systems

Now we'll pivot to the 'Model' and the 'Facets' to examine the lived human experience of the system.

Our human examples

- You're a **peasant**, bound to the land you work. Your lord provides a small plot for your family and theoretical protection, but you owe him days of labor on his fields (corvée), a portion of your harvest, and fees for using his mill or oven. You feel stuck; leaving means starvation or becoming a bandit.

- You're a **young apprentice** in a bustling medieval guild. You dedicate years to learning your craft, working long hours for little pay, often living with your master. You gain skills, but your labor directly enriches the master, and the guild controls your path to becoming independent, demanding loyalty and adherence to its strict rules.

- You're a **minor noble**, loyal to a powerful duke. The duke demands your military service, your knights, and a portion of the taxes you collect from your own meager lands whenever he rides to war or needs funds. You comply, knowing your own status and security depend entirely on his continued favor and protection.

The Human Story

Medieval society created distinct human roles that defined how individuals experienced extraction throughout their lives. These weren't just jobs—they were total social positions that determined your obligations, possibilities, and relationship to power. Each role represented a different way of being caught within the extraction machine, from the bound peasant to the aspiring apprentice to the politically vulnerable minor noble. These roles are the 'Objects' from the Model.

The Peasant: Life Bound to the Land

Model

- **Hierarchy:** Peasant < Lord in deeply asymmetrical relationship based on land tenure, inheritance, and unequal reciprocal obligations, with lord holding ultimate control over land and justice

- **Subject:** Landholding lord

- **Object:** Peasant

- **Resources**: Labor (corvée days on lord's fields), portion of harvest (agricultural produce), fees for using lord's essential services (mill, oven)

- **Methods**: Feudal obligations (serfdom), binding to the land, lord's monopoly over critical infrastructure, lack of economic alternatives (starvation, banditry)

- **Reason/Purpose**: Sustain lord's household/military/political power, ensure agricultural production for entire manor, maintain social order and feudal system

- **Impacts/Consequences**: The peasant lived in perpetual poverty and hard labor, with limited personal freedom and mobility, vulnerable to famine and the lord's arbitrary decisions, lacking opportunity for social advancement while internalizing fatalism

- **Resistance/Contestation**: Passive resistance (slow work, minor sabotage), flight (risky and often illegal), participation in peasant revolts (rare, often brutally suppressed)

Facets

- **Economy & Labor**: Economic survival was engineered through feudal obligations and corvée labor, creating inescapable cycles where agricultural production sustained the lord's power while keeping peasants in perpetual subsistence

- **Shelter & Place**: Physical binding to the land transformed their home territory into a site of extraction, where the very ground they worked became the mechanism of their exploitation and immobility

- **Governance & Power**: Subjection to the lord's absolute authority normalized arbitrary control over justice and daily life, making political powerlessness appear as the natural order rather than imposed domination

- **Community & Relationships**: Shared village obligations created collective dependency structures that both provided mutual support and reinforced acceptance of the feudal system as inevitable social reality

The Young Apprentice: Labor for Learning

Model

- **Hierarchy**: Apprentice < Journeyman < Guild Master in dynamic, asymmetrical hierarchy where apprentice provides years of labor for minimal pay under strict guild control, with promise of future independent status

- **Subject**: Guild Master > Journeyman

- **Object**: Apprentice

- **Resources**: Labor, time, dedication to learning the craft, future economic potential (leveraged for present uncompensated work)

- **Methods**: Long working hours for little to no pay, often living in master's household, strict guild rules controlling training/progression/ eventual independence

- **Reason/Purpose**: Train skilled craftsmen, ensure quality control within craft, provide cheap labor for masters, maintain guild control over trade and membership

- **Impacts/Consequences**: The young apprentice endured years of strenuous work with limited immediate personal gain, dependency on the master, restricted personal freedom, potential for exploitation, but following a rigid path toward independence

- **Resistance/Contestation**: Running away (risky), subtle acts of non-compliance, forming informal bonds with other apprentices for mutual support

Facets

- **Economy & Labor**: Economic dependency was structured through years of uncompensated labor disguised as education, creating extraction cycles where present exploitation was justified by promised future independence

- **Knowledge & Learning Systems**: Educational control channeled skill acquisition through guild monopolies, making professional development inseparable from extended periods of servitude and institutional dependency

- **Culture**: Guild norms and craftsman identity normalized years of harsh working conditions and restricted freedom as the legitimate path to mastery and social respectability

- **Personal & Inner Life**: Psychological adaptation to prolonged subordination through internalized narratives of apprenticeship as character-building journey, obscuring the exploitative nature of unequal labor exchange

The Minor Noble: Caught in the Middle

Model

- **Hierarchy**: Minor Noble as both extractor (from peasants) and extractee (from Duke), positioned in an asymmetrical power relationship within feudal hierarchy

- **Subject**: Minor Noble

- **Object**: Occasionally peasants or those of subordinate classes

- **Resources**: Military service (knights), portion of taxes collected from their own lands (financial resources)

- **Methods**: Demands based on feudal oaths and loyalty, expectation of military aid, implicit threat of losing duke's favor and protection leading to loss of lands or status

- **Reason/Purpose**: Consolidate duke's military strength and financial resources, ensure loyalty and control over domain, fund military campaigns or personal enrichment

- **Impacts/Consequences**: The minor noble faced economic burden on their lands and coffers, constant military readiness, vulnerability to involvement in the duke's conflicts, and dependency on external favor for their own security

- **Resistance/Contestation**: Shifting allegiances to rival lords (dangerous political maneuver), subtle delays or reduced commitment to demands, political maneuvering within court

Facets

- **Governance & Power**: Political positioning within feudal hierarchy created dual extraction relationships where military obligations and loyalty demands made nobles both beneficiaries and victims of the same hierarchical system

- **Economy & Labor**: Financial extraction operated through feudal taxation and military service requirements, making economic security dependent on perpetual readiness to mobilize resources for the duke's interests

- **Community & Relationships**: Feudal bonds normalized obligation-based relationships where personal loyalty became indistinguishable from economic and political dependency, creating social ties that reinforced hierarchical extraction

The Human Experience of Extraction

These three roles reveal how medieval extraction shaped entire lives:

- The **Peasant** experienced the most total extraction—bound to the land, their entire existence revolved around producing for their lord while barely surviving themselves. Their resistance was necessarily covert and small-scale, as open rebellion meant death.

- The **Young Apprentice** lived in a different kind of bondage—voluntary initially, but then locked into years of unpaid labor. Unlike the peasant, they had hope of eventual independence, making their extraction more bearable but also more psychologically complex.

-

- The **Minor Noble** occupied the precarious middle—extracting from those below while being extracted from above. Their political survival required constant navigation of competing loyalties and demands, making them simultaneously exploiter and exploited.

The Patterns Across Roles

Each role was defined by:

- **Asymmetrical relationships** where those above held decisive power

- **Combining material and psychological extraction** - taking both resources and loyalty/submission

- **Limited resistance** - each role found ways to push back within narrow constraints, but resistance was largely discouraged by the civilization itself

- **Embedded social reproduction** - the civilization structure trained people to accept and perpetuate their positions

Medieval society wasn't just an economic system—it was a total way of organizing human lives where your birth determined not just your work, but your entire relationship to power, possibility, and meaning. The extraction wasn't just of labor or resources, but of human potential itself.

That is the holistic view of the extractive systems of Medieval Feudalism & Guild Era and the impact of that extraction upon on the individuals within the system.

But how does this framework apply to contemporary life? Let's consider an example from 'Just Last Week.'

Case Study Two: 'Just Last Week'

Our previous example

> It's 4:15 PM on Tuesday afternoon. Your boss sends an urgent email, telling you that even though your monthly report is due on Friday. The CEO wants it by tomorrow; there's no reason - the CEO just wants to see it. Your heart rate increases. Your blood pressure rises... uuggghhhh... not again... your daughter has soccer practice in 45 minutes. It's either finish and send the report to your boss or take her to practice. Without thinking twice you text to tell her that she'll have to get another ride to practice. This happens frequently enough that you almost expect it... so does she.

Let's apply the framework to a contemporary example. We'll start with the macro/host—the corporate system.

The Corporate Story

Modern corporate culture operates as a sophisticated extraction machine within global capitalism, where companies systematically draw employee time, effort, and personal well-being beyond contracted obligations. At its heart lies the corporation—a profit-driven entity that treats human capital as an infinitely expandable resource, supported by pervasive cultures of urgency and constant availability.

Architecture: Level One - Macro/Host Level

This is the top level—the host or macro system. The Corporation is the primary system operating at this level.

Extractive System: The Corporation

The only top-level system we'll examine in this use case is The Corporation.

Model

The mechanics; how the system acts upon its members.

- **Hierarchy**: CEO and Board at apex, senior management, middle management (your boss), individual employee, with personal life/family below as externalized costs

- **Subjects**: CEO and Board

- **Objects**: Employees, customers

- **Resources**: Employee time/effort, intellectual/emotional labor, personal/family time, mental well-being, physical health, loyalty/dedication

- **Methods**: Top-down urgent demands, implicit pressure prioritizing work over life, constant availability culture, digital communication for instant demands, uncompensated overtime expectations

- **Reason/Purpose**: Maximize corporate output/efficiency, ensure immediate leadership responsiveness, maintain high performance image, achieve financial targets by extracting maximum human capital value

- **Impacts/Consequences**: A modern corporation systematically extracts employee time, effort, dedication, and personal sacrifices—often beyond contracted hours and compensation—for corporate objectives, leading to burnout, chronic stress, strained relationships, eroded boundaries, and decreased satisfaction

- **Resistance/Contestation**: Internalized frustration, resignation, passive resistance (quiet quitting, reduced engagement), seeking alternative employment, advocating for work-life balance policies

Facets

The psychological-material, sociocultural apparatus that operates through archetypal conditioning across all life domains.

- **Governance & Power**: Organizational hierarchies systematically translate arbitrary executive demands into non-negotiable employee directives, normalizing top-down control as legitimate management while obscuring the extractive nature of unlimited authority over worker time and priorities

- **Economy & Labor**: Salaried compensation models engineered systematic unpaid overtime extraction by creating fixed-pay structures that incentivize maximum labor extraction while disguising wage theft as professional expectation and career advancement opportunity

- **Culture**: Corporate devotion ideology normalized work-above-all mentalities that transformed personal sacrifice into moral virtue, making constant availability and family neglect appear as professional dedication rather than exploitative boundary violation

- **Religion & Spirituality**: Quasi-religious corporate loyalty created sacred obligations to sacrifice personal well-being for organizational goals, making employee exploitation indistinguishable from spiritual calling and moral duty to the corporate mission

- **Knowledge & Learning**: Professional development systems condition employees to internalize intrusion patterns as career necessities, making adaptation to exploitative demands appear as skill-building rather than psychological conditioning to accept boundary violations

- **Tools & Technology**: Digital communication infrastructure enables instant workplace intrusion into personal time and private spaces, making 24/7 availability appear as technological convenience rather than systematic erosion of life boundaries

- **Personal & Inner Life**: Direct extraction of mental peace and emotional well-being through constant stress and urgency demands, normalizing chronic anxiety and burnout as the price of professional success and economic security

- **Community & Relationships**: Systematic destruction of family commitments and social reliability through unpredictable work demands, making relationship erosion appear as individual time management failure rather than structural extraction of social bonds

- **Shelter & Place**: Transformation of homes into sites of work anxiety and demand response through mortgage dependency and remote work expectations, making private domestic space inseparable from corporate extraction territory

Architecture: Level Two - Paraextractive Systems

This is the second level of the system architecture. In this example, the modern corporate paradigm operates through a sophisticated cultural paraextractive system.

Paraextractive System: The Culture of Urgency - Semi-Autonomous Behavioral System

Model

- **Hierarchy**: Implicit behavioral hierarchy where perceived urgency overrides individual autonomy and structured workflows, parallel to formal reporting

- **Subjects**: Corporate leaders, though this is largely an unconscious sociocultural pattern

- **Objects**: Working professionals, employees

- **Resources**: Employee ability to plan/manage time, sense of work control, freedom from interruption, emotional equilibrium

- **Methods**: Frequent 'urgent' demands from all levels, lack of pushback consequences, constant digital communication implying immediate response, normalized after-hours work

- **Reason/Purpose**: Maintain agile/responsive workforce, create high productivity perception, justify arbitrary senior leadership demands

- **Impacts/Consequences**: A pervasive, self-reinforcing set of norms demanding immediate responsiveness that prioritizes perceived urgency over planned work or personal life, extracting spontaneity, boundaries, and calm

- **Resistance/Contestation**: Internalized frustration, passive resistance (delayed responses when non-critical), collective process improvement advocacy

Facets

- **Culture**: Urgency ideology systematically extracts planned workflow and autonomous time management through manufactured crisis atmospheres that normalize reactive behavior as professional competence, making constant interruption appear as organizational agility rather than systematic destruction of structured work capacity

- **Personal & Inner Life**: Continuous anticipation systems engineer chronic stress responses through perpetual 'on-call' psychological states, creating extraction cycles where inner peace and emotional equilibrium became sacrificed to maintain readiness for arbitrary urgent demands disguised as workplace responsiveness

Architecture: Level Three - Subextractive Systems

This layer embodies the active enforcement mechanisms of the layers above. The First and Second Layers require an agent brandishing their authority to actualize their imperatives. This layer coordinates extraction.

Subextractive System: The Boss - Corporate Agent

Model

- **Hierarchy**: Immediate manager positioned directly above employee, acting as point of contact and enforcer of corporate demands

- **Subjects**: Middle managers

- **Objects**: Anyone further down the org chart

- **Resources**: Employee immediate labor, willingness to forgo personal commitments, emotional stress capacity, loyalty

- **Methods**: Direct urgent email commands, leveraging positional authority, conveying CEO demand importance, creating urgency/obligation for immediate compliance

- **Reason/Purpose**: Fulfill CEO's arbitrary demands for the Corporation, ensure positive superior performance view, maintain efficiency by pushing burden to subordinates

- **Impacts/Consequences**: Your immediate manager directly enforces corporate demands, extracting immediate compliance, extra effort, and personal sacrifice to fulfill corporate directives

- **Resistance/Contestation**: Employee internal monologue ("uuggghhhh...") as passive mental resistance reflecting frustration without overt expression

Facets

- **Governance & Power**: Managerial authority systematically extracts employee autonomy through positional leverage that transforms arbitrary corporate demands into non-negotiable personal obligations, making hierarchical coercion appear as legitimate workplace communication rather than direct exploitation of power imbalances

- **Economy & Labor**: Direct labor extraction operates through immediate demand fulfillment expectations that prioritize corporate urgency over contracted work boundaries, making unpaid overtime and personal time sacrifice appear as professional responsibility rather than wage theft through authority pressure

- **Tools & Technology**: Email communication infrastructure enables unavoidable demand delivery that bypasses normal workflow processes, making instant compliance extraction appear as efficient management communication rather than systematic boundary violation through technological coercion

- **Personal & Inner Life**: Physiological stress induction through authority-backed urgent demands directly extracts mental well-being and emotional equilibrium, making chronic anxiety responses appear as natural workplace pressure rather than deliberate extraction of psychological peace through hierarchical intimidation

Subextractive System: Employee's Internalized Expectations - Self-Extraction System

Model

- **Hierarchy**: Internalized, self-imposed hierarchy where perceived corporate demands override individual desire for personal time/ boundaries

- **Subject**: Your unconscious self

- **Object**: Your conscious self

- **Resources**: Employee free will, ability to say 'no', family time, mental peace, self-worth outside work

- **Methods**: Automatic work demand prioritization, immediate emotional task response, inevitable personal sacrifice assumption, corporate demand rationalization happening 'without thinking twice'

- **Reason/Purpose**: Avoid perceived negative consequences (poor reviews, job insecurity, being labeled difficult), conform to corporate norms, maintain professional identity, alleviate immediate stress through quick compliance

- **Impacts/Consequences**: The employee's learned behavior and psychological adaptation to corporate culture extracts personal agency, boundaries, and emotional well-being through self-imposed compliance

- **Resistance/Contestation**: Internal "uuggghhhh…" as brief, unexpressed resistance before compliance

Facets

- **Culture**: Internalized corporate ideology systematically extracts autonomous decision-making through automatic boundary surrender mechanisms (normalized 'without thinking twice' compliance) making self-sacrifice appear as professional instinct rather than conditioned response to exploitative workplace expectations

- **Personal & Inner Life**: Psychological conditioning systems directly extract personal agency and emotional well-being through immediate stress responses that prioritize corporate demands over individual needs, making family time sacrifice appear as natural responsibility rather than systematic erosion of personal autonomy

- **Knowledge & Learning**: Learned compliance patterns engineer self-extraction cycles through internalized non-negotiable expectations that transform employees into their own exploitation agents, making voluntary boundary violation appear as professional competence rather than psychological conditioning to corporate control mechanisms

The Pattern of Modern Extraction

Corporate extraction works through normalization (making constant availability feel normal), internalization (employees policing themselves), and technological intrusion (digital tools eliminating boundaries). Unlike medieval systems that relied on legal bondage, modern corporate extraction operates through psychological conditioning and economic fear—the mortgage that must be paid, the career that might be damaged.

The most devious aspect is how employees become complicit in their own extraction, developing internalized expectations that make resistance feel impossible. The system doesn't just take your time—it takes your ability to imagine saying no.

This isn't just about work-life balance—it's about a total system that transforms human beings into infinitely available resources for corporate objectives, extracting not just labor but the very capacity for autonomous living.

The Human in the System

This system creates a reality where employees automatically sacrifice personal boundaries, family commitments, and mental well-being for corporate demands. The extraction is so complete that resistance becomes internal and fleeting—a brief "uuggghhhh..." before compliance. Even family members learn to expect disappointment, showing how corporate extraction overrides intimate relationships.

The Human Story

The modern employee represents a new form of human subjugation within corporate capitalism—one that appears voluntary but operates through sophisticated psychological and economic coercion. Unlike medieval peasants bound by law or apprentices bound by contract, the employee is bound by mortgage payments, career advancement fears, and internalized expectations of constant availability.

The Modern Employee: Always-On, Never Enough - Existing Within Corporate Extraction

Model

- **Hierarchy**: CEO > Boss > Employee in asymmetrical power dynamic where employee's personal time and family obligations are consistently overridden by arbitrary, last-minute work demands without additional compensation. The Boss extracts, but is also extracted from

- **Subjects**: Everyone above the employee

- **Object**: The employee themselves

- **Resources**: Personal time, family time, mental peace, emotional well-being (stress, rising blood pressure)

- **Methods**: Urgent emails outside standard work hours, arbitrary deadlines ("CEO wants it by tomorrow"), implicit expectation of constant availability and work prioritization

- **Reason/Purpose**: Maximize corporate productivity and responsiveness, fulfill management's immediate desires without considering employee work-life balance or well-being

- **Impacts/Consequences**: The modern employee experiences increased stress and anxiety, erosion of work-life boundaries, neglect of personal and family obligations, potential burnout, and normalization of unhealthy work patterns, creating cognitive dissonance from valuing family while repeatedly sacrificing it

- **Resistance/Contestation**: Setting boundaries (often with perceived career risk), 'quiet quitting' or disengagement, seeking work environments with better work-life balance, advocating for 'right to disconnect' legislation

Facets

- **Personal & Inner Life**: Systematic extraction of emotional well-being and family relationships through chronic stress induction and cognitive dissonance creation, where employees internalize the contradiction between valuing family while repeatedly sacrificing it to arbitrary corporate demands disguised as professional necessity

- **Economy & Labor**: Uncompensated labor extraction operate through salary structures that enable unlimited work hour expansion into personal time, making unpaid overtime appear as career investment rather than systematic wage theft through boundary erosion and availability expectations

- **Tools & Technology**: Digital communication infrastructure systematically extracts personal time and private space through instant connectivity demands that transform phones and laptops into corporate leashes, making 24/7 accessibility appear as technological convenience rather than systematic annexation of domestic life and mental freedom

- **Culture**: Always-on corporate ideology systematically extracts autonomous decision-making through pervasive "can't-say-no" mentalities that normalize constant availability as a professional virtue, making personal boundary violation appear as dedication rather than conditioned surrender to exploitative workplace expectations

The Human Experience of Modern Extraction

The employee's position reveals how contemporary extraction has evolved beyond medieval systems:

- **Psychological Sophistication**: Unlike the peasant's legal bondage or the apprentice's contractual obligation, the employee's extraction operates through internalized expectations. The "uuggghhhh…" followed by immediate compliance shows how resistance has been reduced to momentary internal frustration before automatic submission.

- **Technology as Control**: Email transforms the home from refuge into potential workplace, making extraction possible 24/7. The medieval lord needed bailiffs to oversee peasant labor; the modern corporation uses digital technology to make employees monitor themselves.

- **Family as Collateral**: The employee's daughter learning to expect disappointment shows how corporate extraction colonizes intimate relationships. Medieval extraction took labor; modern extraction takes the capacity for reliable family presence.

- **Economic Coercion**: The fear of not paying the mortgage creates compliance more effectively than medieval legal bondage. The employee chooses their subjugation daily, but within a system that makes alternatives feel impossible.

The Paradox of Modern Freedom

The employee's situation reveals the sophisticated evolution of extraction systems:

- **Apparent Choice**: Unlike serfs, employees can theoretically quit—but economic necessity and career concerns make this choice largely illusory

- **Internalized Control**: The most effective extraction happens when employees police themselves, automatically prioritizing work demands 'without thinking twice'

- **Normalized Sacrifice**: The phrase "this happens frequently enough that you almost expect it" shows how extraordinary demands become ordinary expectations

- **Invisible Boundaries**: Work and life blend seamlessly—through the devices we carry, making resistance harder to locate and organize

The Pattern of Contemporary Extraction

The modern employee experiences extraction through:

- **Temporal Appropriation**: Every moment becomes potentially claimable by corporate demands

- **Emotional Labor**: Not just time and energy, but mental peace and family relationships become corporate resources

- **Self-Surveillance**: Employees internalize corporate needs, making external monitoring less necessary

- **Manufactured Urgency**: Arbitrary deadlines create artificial crises that justify boundary violations

The modern corporate employee represents the perfect model of extraction— the system so thoroughly internalized that resistance feels selfish, unrealistic, or career-limiting. Unlike medieval peasants who knew they were oppressed, modern employees often blame themselves for their inability to 'balance' unlimited corporate demands with finite personal resources.

This isn't just about work-life balance—it's about a total system that has learned to extract human life itself while making its victims feel grateful for the opportunity.

A Flexible Framework for Examining Extraction

These case studies demonstrate the Architecture, Model, and Facets framework's analytical versatility, transitioning seamlessly from Medieval Feudalism & Guilds to contemporary pressures in the 'Just Last Week' example.

For historical analysis, the Architecture exposed feudalism's overt extractions—revealing the Church as a Paraextractive System and bailiffs as Subextractive agents. The Model and Facets mapped explicit hierarchies and resource demands, while The Human Story illuminated their physical and psychological impacts on individuals from a ground-level perspective.

In contemporary contexts, the framework revealed the workings of corporate environments as Host Systems extracting labor, time, and well-being. It identifies invisible patterns like 'Culture of Urgency' as Paraextractive forces demanding constant availability, and highlights 'self-extraction' as a Subextractive System where internalized expectations erode personal agency.

Whether analyzing ancient land taxes or urgent emails, the framework's Architecture operating through the core elements of the Model remains applicable. The Facets illuminate the key domains within any extractive system.

This analytical lens reveals a crucial insight: while extraction evolves from physical coercion to psychological pressure, the underlying mechanisms of concentrating control persist. Medieval peasants knew their bondage explicitly; modern employees face 'hustle porn' that disguises self-extraction as self-actualization, making resistance feel like personal failure rather than systemic critique.

Beyond historical analysis, this framework reveals how the collective psyche shapes individual experience across historical contexts. It enables a feeling-toned examination of archetypal power and extractive patterns embedded in the collective unconscious. For contemporary issues, the framework gauges extraction's psychic layers through hierarchical systems, explaining why seemingly minor disturbances carry unexpectedly powerful emotional charges.

Part II |
The Dormant Soul Complex

A modern complex

A Primer on Jung's Concepts

Carl Jung, I'd assert, is the father of Western Psychology. In his day, although considered reputable, he was also perceived as a bit too mystic; too esoteric; too unconventional. Jung spoke in symbols, in myth, in archetypes, mandalas, and synchronicities. He valued intuition as much as logic. He was a distinguished cartographer and explorer of internal and external psychological landscapes.

Unless you're an ouroboros-inked Jungian or a scholar who has pursued the rich field of Jungian thought, his concepts may be new to you. Jung's ideas about personal and collective psychological evolution have influenced psychology for over a century, yet his concepts often feel abstract or anachronistic to modern readers. I've been influenced by his concepts since my first year of college, when I first read *Memories, Dreams, Reflections* (1961). I've also grappled with understanding them. This primer attempts to demystify his fundamental concepts for readers facing similar challenges. These terms are not my own, but I've distilled them into more approachable terminology, articulated in the way I understand them.

Mapping the Jungian Psyche

Jung's model of the individual psyche is often described as a layered structure contained within The Self, which extends far beyond the conscious mind. It consists of three fundamental components and many other subcomponents:

- **The Self**: The ultimate and most important archetype, the Self is the unifying center of the entire psyche. It represents the autonomic striving for psychological wholeness and integration. It is the overarching organizing principle that encompasses both the conscious and unconscious mind. While the Ego is the center of consciousness, the Self is both center and the container of the total psyche.

- **The Ego**: The Ego is what you think of as 'I.' This is the center of consciousness. It is your sense of self, your identity, and your awareness of the world. Its primary function is to mediate between the conscious mind and both the external world and the unconscious.

  - **The Persona**: A key component of the Ego, the Persona is the social mask we wear in public—the collection of social roles, behaviors, and expectations we adopt to fit into society. It is the outer expression of our personality, often hiding the deeper layers of the self.

    Example: A person who is known as the 'life of the party' and a social butterfly, always cracking jokes and entertaining friends. In private, however, they are a quiet, introspective individual who prefers solitude and deeply values serious conversations. The outgoing persona is a facade they adopt for social situations.

- **The Personal Unconscious**: This is a vast, personal hidden storehouse of everything that was once conscious but has been forgotten, repressed, or subliminally perceived. It includes forgotten memories, suppressed emotions, and unacknowledged thoughts. It is the birthplace of your own complexes—clusters of emotionally charged ideas and images that have been pushed out of consciousness but can still influence behavior and perception.

- **The Shadow**: A key archetype within the Personal Unconscious, the Shadow is the dark, repressed, and unacknowledged side of the self. It comprises of all the instincts, desires, and behaviors that the Ego deems unacceptable. While often seen as negative, the Shadow also contains creative and vital energy that is essential for psychological growth if integrated consciously. As Jung famously stated, "Until you make the unconscious conscious, it will direct your life and you will call it fate," emphasizing the powerful influence of the shadow.

  Example: An individual who prides themselves on being a kind and generous person, but secretly harbors feelings of jealousy and resentment toward a successful friend. The shadow is the unacknowledged side of their personality that contains these unacceptable emotions.

- **The Collective Unconscious**: This is the deepest, most inaccessible layer of the psyche. It is not personal to the individual but is shared by all of humanity. It is an inherited, universal blueprint that contains primordial archetypes, images, and instincts. The DNA of our meaning-making, purpose-seeking self.

  Example: People from vastly different cultures who have never met might still have the same spontaneous and intense fear of snakes, even if they have never encountered a venomous one. This suggests a shared, inherited psychic pattern.

- **Archetype**: A fundamental part of the Collective Unconscious. An archetype is a primordial, inherited pattern of thought and behavior. It is a psychic blueprint that is common to all humanity and manifests in symbolic forms in myths, dreams, folklore, and religion, shaping our experiences and reactions to the world. The Collective Unconscious speaks through these symbolic images, e.g., the Hero, the Mother, the Maiden, the Crone, or the Wise Old Man.

The map of the Individual Psyche, with its layers of Ego and unconscious material, provides the essential framework for understanding our internal world. Yet, as this map suggests, no Psyche exists in isolation. The Individual Psyche, centered around the Ego and ultimately the Self, is inextricably nested within the larger psychological landscape of the group. To truly comprehend the modern Self and its struggles, its strengths, and its vulnerabilities—we must also understand the powerful, shaping forces of the Collective. The Collective Unconscious, for instance, is not only a part of your Individual Psyche but also a part of the Collective Psyche itself—because you are an active member of that collective.

The Topography of The Collective

The **Collective**, in this context, refers to the shared psychological reality of a group. It is the communal mind that holds the collective's beliefs, values, and norms, as well as its historical memories, myths, and unconscious parts.

Émile Durkheim, in his foundational work *The Division of Labour in Society*, introduced the concept of the Collective Consciousness in 1893. Jung followed by publishing his first major work on the Collective Unconscious, *Wandlungen und Symbole der Libido* (Symbols of Transformation), in 1912. Durkheim, a sociologist, examined the external system's framework—the shared norms, laws, and public ideals that glue a society together. Jung explored the psychological experience of that framework—its inner awareness—the psychological contents that come from living within that collective.

Building upon the foundational work of Durkheim and Jung, contemporary thinkers such as Thomas Singer, Andrew Samuels, and Joseph Cambray have continued to explore the complex relationship between the Individual and the Collective. They have sought to understand how the Collective has transformed in our hyperconnected, technologically-saturated world—how psychic material 'goes viral.' By extending these original concepts, post-Jungian scholars provide us with the tools to analyze the Collective's influence on our contemporary psychic landscape. The Collective serves as the container—the vast, overarching psychological reality that determines the range of possibilities, myths, and struggles shared by every Individual nested within it. With this understanding of the nested Psyche, we can now map the parts of the modern Collective that are most relevant to understanding our current psychological state.

The Collective

The Collective Conscious: The shared psychological reality of the group, which holds its common beliefs, values, and norms. This is the 'rational veneer' that defines what is publicly acceptable and actively manages the group's public identity. In our context, it is the collective's awareness of its own systems, policies, and ideals, even if those are a convenient fiction.

> **Example**: The widely accepted belief in a society that 'bigger is better,' influencing everything from the size of cars and houses to the goals of corporations, even if that belief is a fiction that masks a deeper hunger for fulfillment.

The Collective Persona (A Jungian-Derived Concept): This is the public face or mask that a collective projects to the world. It is a curated facade designed to project a specific image and to conform to the expectations of a social role. The

Collective Persona helps us understand the psychological dynamics of groups, organizations, and nations.

> **Example**: A nation that promotes itself as a beacon of freedom and democracy on the world stage, while simultaneously engaging in acts of surveillance or economic exploitation that contradict that public image.

The Collective Shadow: The dark, repressed, and destructive side of the group. It is the repository for all the instincts and behaviors a society deems unacceptable. When the Collective's persona and consciousness can no longer contain this shadow, it can erupt with staggering power. The constant interaction between the Collective Persona and the Collective Shadow creates a state of perpetual psychological tension.

> **Example**: A historical event, such as an unresolved genocide or systemic oppression, that a nation's collective consciousness has repressed or denied. This unacknowledged history can later erupt in the form of widespread social unrest, political polarization, or violent conflict.

Foundational Ley Lines

Having knowledge of the individual and collective psyches, we can move to the foundational ley lines that define their states of imbalance and drive hidden behavior. A psyche out of alignment can manifest as a specific psychic structure or a pervasive state of suffering. These core Individual imbalances, though personal, are often constellated by collective forces through their Collective counterparts. Through their syntonic, symbiotic relationships the Collective variants influence Individual psyche nearly invisibly through the unconscious. This is how Collective becomes Individual.

Individual and Collective Complexes: An **Individual Complex** is a cluster of emotionally charged ideas, images, and memories that has been pushed from the conscious mind yet continues to exert a hidden, powerful influence on a person's thoughts, emotions, and behavior. A **Collective Complex** is a similar cluster of emotionally charged historical events, cultural memories, or shared images that operates autonomously within a group, influencing its shared beliefs, behaviors, and identity.

> **Example - Individual Complex:** A person who, as a child, was frequently told they were 'not smart enough' by a sibling may develop an 'inferiority complex' around intellectual tasks. As an adult, they might avoid challenging situations at work or downplay their own intelligence, even when they are capable and knowledgeable.

> **Example - Collective Complex:** A community that has been shaped by a collective trauma, such as a natural disaster or a factory closure, may develop a powerful 'trauma complex.' This can lead the group to view all new opportunities with suspicion and resist change, even if it is beneficial, because their shared identity is now defined by their past suffering.

Individual and Collective Neuroses: An **Individual Neurosis** is a state of psychological suffering caused by a lack of wholeness and a disjunction between the conscious and unconscious parts of the psyche. It is a psychic imbalance that signals a need for the conscious mind to re-establish a relationship with its repressed or ignored contents. A **Collective Neurosis** is a state of widespread psychic dis-ease or suffering within a society or group caused by a fundamental lack of wholeness.

> **Example - Individual Neurosis:** A highly anxious person who engages in compulsive behaviors to manage their fear of uncertainty. Their unconscious mind is attempting to compensate for the Ego's one-sided obsession with control.

> **Example - Collective Neurosis:** The sudden mass hysteria in a society in response to an unsubstantiated conspiracy theory, leading to a breakdown of rational discourse and widespread irrational fear.

The Dynamic Interplay

The psychological landscape is not a static map but a dynamic field where the Individual and the Collective are in constant, powerful interaction. It is within this field that the foundational fault lines we have just defined are animated. The following are the key psychological processes that govern this interplay—a field of forces that can either lead to profound self-discovery or, if left unexamined, to the erosion of the authentic self.

- **Circumambulation:** The non-linear, circular process of approaching a psychic center, most commonly the Self (the archetype of wholeness). A concept borrowed from religious ritual, it describes the method of development where the individual moves around the central core of their Self, repeatedly engaging with and integrating various facets of the unconscious (symbols, complexes, and archetypes) to gain a more complete understanding. Often used to refer to the process of Individuation.

- **Telos:** The inherent final aim or purpose that drives the development of the Psyche. A concept borrowed from Aristotelian philosophy, it describes the goal-directedness (teleology) of the Unconscious, asserting that psychic life is not merely a consequence of past events (causality), but is always striving toward a unique, future state of completion and wholeness.

- **Libido**: In Jung's work, libido is not strictly sexual energy, as in Freud's theories. Instead, it's a broader term for the general psychic energy that powers all psychological processes and gives them their force and vitality. It is the vital energy that drives a person's thoughts, emotions, and motivations. All of the dynamics described below are powered by the movement and flow of this energy.

- **Constellation**: The process by which a dormant archetype or complex is activated and energized by an external event or situation. It brings a previously unconscious psychic content into a state of heightened affective charge, causing it to become active in the conscious mind. This explains how a seemingly small event can trigger a disproportionately powerful psychic response.

  Example: A person who grew up with a narcissistic parent, who made them feel worthless, may carry a dormant 'inferiority complex.' A seemingly small negative comment during a review from a boss can constellate this complex, triggering a disproportionate emotional spiral that goes far beyond the scope of the feedback.

- **Amplification**: The intensification of a constellated psychic content through association with universal symbols, myths, or narratives. While Jung originally used this term for a therapeutic process, in a collective context, describes how digital media and social narratives can intensify a constellated complex far beyond its original scope, turning a personal trigger into a collective contagion.

  Example: A minor incident at a local park, such as a child's toy not being shared, is recounted as a story of aggression and disrespect by a neighborhood figure. As the story is shared and exaggerated, it taps into the community's underlying anxieties about safety and social decay. The simple act of an unshared toy is amplified into a sign of a looming community crisis, leading to a widespread feeling of anxiety and distrust among residents that is entirely disproportionate to the original event.

- **Projection**: An unconscious psychological mechanism where a person attributes a disowned part of themselves—particularly their unintegrated Shadow—to someone or something else. On a collective level, this mechanism allows a group to project its own dark impulses onto an 'other'— a scapegoat, a rival, or a villain.

Example: A person who secretly harbors intense anger but cannot consciously admit it might constantly perceive others as hostile or aggressive, believing the hostility originates from them, when in reality, it's a projection of their own repressed anger.

- **Inflation and Deflation**: Inflation is the expansion of the Ego beyond its proper boundaries, caused by its identification with a powerful archetype from the Collective Unconscious or with a Collective Persona—resulting in a distorted sense of self marked by grandiosity and a false sense of invulnerability. The inevitable consequence is deflation, the painful and humbling collapse of the inflated Ego, forcing a re-engagement with one's human limitations.

  Example - Inflation: A musician who achieves sudden and widespread fame begins to believe their own hype, developing a sense of superiority and entitlement. They start making outlandish demands and acting without regard for consequences.

  Example - Deflation: An online spiritual guru who built a massive following on a foundation of false promises and a charismatic persona is exposed as a fraud. The humiliating public downfall and loss of their entire community forces them to confront the limitations of their actual self.

- **Entrainment**: The process by which a person's psychological or emotional state synchronizes with a rhythmic external source. In the modern context, this can be seen in how the constant, repetitive feedback loops of social media and news cycles subtly impose a collective emotional rhythm—be it outrage, anxiety, or celebration—on the individual psyche, compelling them to align with the collective's feeling state.

Example: At a political rally, an individual finds their personal energy and breathing begin to align with the rhythmic chanting and clapping of the crowd. They feel a powerful sense of belonging and shared purpose that is directly synchronized with the group's collective rhythm.

- **Enantiodromia**: Jung borrowed this principle from the ancient Greek philosopher Heraclitus. It states that when any one-sided tendency is pushed to its extreme, it will inevitably turn into its opposite. This is a crucial balancing principle of the psyche. For example, a one-sided Collective Persona or an inflated Ego, having become overly identified with a specific attitude, is destined to collapse and be replaced by its polar opposite.

    Example: A high-performing employee who, after years of extreme corporate dedication and constant availability, suddenly shifts to doing only the bare minimum required by their job description, refusing overtime and after-hours communications, resulting in quiet quitting.

- **Compensation**: The autonomic function of the psyche. It is the unconscious providing what is missing from the conscious mind to create balance. When the conscious attitude is one-sided (e.g., overly rational, overly optimistic, or conforming to a Persona), the unconscious will generate compensating material in dreams, fantasies, or impulsive behavior to correct the imbalance.

    Example: A person who is overly rational and emotionally repressed in their waking life might dream of being overwhelmed by a giant, dark wave or expressing intense anger, compensating for their one-sided conscious attitude.

- **The Transcendent Function**: The psychological function that emerges from the tension between conscious and unconscious material. This dynamic process actively synthesizes two opposing positions (thesis and antithesis) into a third, new attitude or symbol (synthesis). It is the psyche's engine for creating new, forward-moving meaning and is the core mechanism that leads to psychological transformation. It is often experienced subjectively as a 'third way,' a sudden insight, or a symbol that resolves a previously paralyzing internal conflict.

  Example: A person is torn between the conscious desire for a secure but boring job and the unconscious urge for a risky but fulfilling artistic career. The Transcendent Function might generate a dream of building a creative side business that eventually allows them to transition—resolving the tension into a new, progressive path forward that neither the conscious Ego nor the unconscious alone could devise.

- **Autonomous Functioning**: The independent, un-willed action of a complex or archetype. When a complex is constellated, it can temporarily take on an autonomous life of its own, seizing control of the Ego and compelling behavior without conscious direction. This explains why an individual might feel 'taken over' by an intense emotional reaction or an uncharacteristic outburst. It is how a complex 'has us' instead of 'us having a complex'.

  Example: A person who feels 'possessed' by an intense rage, unable to control their words or actions in a moment of fury, only to feel bewildered by their own behavior afterward.

- **Participation Mystique**: A state of psychic identification where the individual's ego is not differentiated from the group or an object. It is a pre-conscious, non-rational fusion of subject and object. In the modern world, this is a key dynamic of crowd behavior and tribalism, where a person can lose their individual perspective and become unconsciously swept up in the will and emotions of the collective.

  Example: A person becomes so identified with a specific car brand that their ego is completely fused with its image of rugged individualism and freedom. They might irrationally defend the company's decisions online, viewing any criticism of the brand as a personal attack. Their identity is so intertwined with the brand that their capacity for objective judgment is lost.

The Soul

The concept of the 'soul' is complex, deeply personal, and often feels more like a lived experience than a defined term. In my framework the soul is both a philosophical foundation and a dynamic component of the psyche.

My Own View

In my view, the 'soul' is the lived experience of 'isness'—a state of embodied presence that transcends yet contains all the functions of the mind, emotion, and body. It is the point where internal meets external; where tension finds harmony; and where action meets stillness. It is the sum of 'you' becoming even more 'you'—the eternal moment where memory and the future coalesce into the now.

My perspective is deeply influenced by post-Jungian thinkers such as Donald Kalsched, who saw the soul's vulnerable core and protective mechanisms of trauma; Marion Woodman, who saw the soul blooming through all experiences; and James Hillman, who viewed it not as a thing inside us, but as a reflective perspective that mediates events and makes meaning possible.

Jung's Perspective

Carl Jung's definition of the 'soul' (often synonymous with the 'psyche') was not static. He saw it as a complex and multifaceted totality, extending beyond a simple spiritual or religious definition. Jung explored this concept extensively in his works, particularly in *The Archetypes and the Collective Unconscious* (Volume 9i) and *The Structure and Dynamics of the Psyche* (Volume 8).

Key Aspects of Jung's Concept of Soul

The Totality of the Psyche: For Jung, the 'soul' or 'psyche' refers to the entire realm of the human mind, encompassing both the conscious and unconscious. As he wrote, "By psyche I understand the totality of all psychic processes, conscious and unconscious" (CW 6, § 765).

113

Psychological Experience of the Body: Jung viewed the soul as the psychological experience of the body. He suggested that symptomatic expressions of the body are a natural attempt at healing, a view that aligns profoundly with the modern concept of somatic experience. Jung saw the body not just as a physical container but as a gateway to the unconscious—where physical sensations and symptoms can be symbolic expressions of deeper psychological issues.

> **Example**: A person experiencing chronic back pain that doctors cannot diagnose may find relief when they address a deep-seated psychological issue. Their back is literally and figuratively 'carrying the weight' of an unresolved emotional burden, which their unconscious is attempting to express through the body.

Spiritual Dimension: Jung believed the soul has an inherent spiritual dimension, representing a person's connection to something greater than themselves. This connection is expressed through meaning, purpose, and creativity. In *Modern Man in Search of a Soul* (1933), he directly addressed this point:

> "I am accused of mysticism. I do not, however, hold myself responsible for the fact that man has, everywhere and always, spontaneously developed religious forms of expression, and that the human psyche from time immemorial has been shot through with religious feelings and ideas. Whoever cannot see this aspect of the human psyche is blind, and whoever chooses to explain it away, or to 'enlighten' it away, has no sense of reality."

The Religious Function: This is the psyche's innate and autonomous drive to find meaning and to connect with something greater than the ego. For Jung, this is an instinct as fundamental as hunger or sexuality and acts on behalf of the soul. It is not about a specific religion but is a primary psychological need that seeks a relationship with the numinous and gives life its purpose.

Example: An agnostic person finds profound meaning and connection to something greater than themselves by spending time in nature. The regular practice of hiking and observing the changing seasons serves their innate psychological need for ritual and purpose, acting as a 'religious function' in their life.

The Individuation Process: The soul is central to Jung's concept of individuation, the lifelong process of becoming a whole and integrated self. This involves the conscious integration of all psychic material—including the shadow, anima/animus, and other archetypes—into the totality of the personality, culminating in the realization of the Self.

Distinction from 'Spirit': While often used interchangeably, Jung sometimes differentiated the soul from the spirit. He saw the soul as more grounded, connected to the body, emotions, and the imaginative realm. The spirit, in contrast, tends to be more abstract, carrying one off into ethereal realms. For Jung, the soul's function is to keep us grounded and conscious, providing a 'discriminative function' in our lives.

Example: An academic's pursuit of a purely intellectual and abstract philosophical idea that leads them away from embodied life and relationships is a function of the spirit. In contrast, the artist's engagement with raw, embodied emotion and the physical act of creation to express their personal truth is a function of the soul.

In His Own Words

The best way to understand the dynamic, living nature of the soul is through Jung's personal insights from his autobiography, *Memories, Dreams, Reflections* (1961). His own words powerfully capture the essence of his own perspective:

> "Our souls as well as our bodies are composed of individual elements which were already present in the ranks of our ancestors. The 'newness' in the individual psyche is an endlessly varied recombination of age-old components."

> "People will do anything, no matter how absurd, to avoid facing their own souls."

> "The dream is a little hidden door in the innermost and most secret recesses of the soul, opening into that cosmic night which was psyche long before there was any ego-consciousness."

> "Learn your theories as well as you can, but put them aside when you touch the miracle of the living soul."

In short, for Jung, the soul is the dynamic force that unites individual experience with universal patterns in the search for wholeness.

Archetypes and Symbols

Having mapped the structures and dynamics of the individual and collective psyche, we'll explore the language they speak: archetypes and symbols. If the psyche is a vast and intricate landscape, then archetypes are its primordial inhabitants and symbols are the living, dynamic signs that point the way to meaning. These two concepts are central to understanding Jung's views on how the unconscious communicates and how the collective shapes the individual. In the following section, we will examine these universal patterns and their expressions as they form the very bedrock of our psychological experience.

Archetypes

Archetypes are universal, archaic symbols and images that derive from and reside in the collective unconscious. They are the 'primordial images' or 'dominants of the collective unconscious.' As the psychic counterpart of instinct, archetypes are innate, symbolic, psychological expressions that manifest in response to patterned biological instincts. They are impersonal and formless, transcending culture and geography, yet expressing themselves in a vast array of images and behaviors within particular cultures. Archetypes form a common foundation for the experiences of all humans, with each individual building their unique experiences on top of this universal substrate.

> **Example**: The universal "hero's journey" narrative that appears in nearly every culture's myths, from ancient folklore to modern blockbusters. This shared pattern suggests a deeper, innate blueprint for stories about transformation and overcoming challenges.

Symbols

Jung considered symbols to be fundamental to the human psyche, serving as the primary language of the unconscious and vital bridges between the conscious and unconscious realms. Unlike mere signs (which have fixed meanings), Jungian symbols are dynamic, alive, and multi-layered, carrying a richness of meaning that cannot be fully grasped by rational thought alone.

- **Language of the Unconscious**: Symbols are how the unconscious communicates with the conscious mind, especially through dreams, fantasies, and creative expressions. They speak in images, not logical propositions.

- **Bridging Conscious and Unconscious**: Symbols serve as mediators, allowing the ego to connect with deeper, often irrational, contents of the personal and collective unconscious. They make otherwise inaccessible psychic material available to consciousness.

  Example: A dream image of a dragon doesn't just mean 'danger' (a sign). It might symbolize a repressed, powerful instinctual drive, a challenging obstacle in one's life, or even a hidden treasure, embodying a tension of opposites (destructive and protective, primitive and wise).

- **Holding Opposites** (Coincidentia Oppositorum): True symbols have the unique capacity to unite contradictory or opposing aspects of experience within a single image. This inherent paradox is central to their transformative power.

  Example: The mandala (a symbol of the Self) often depicts a circle and a square, representing the integration of psychic wholeness (circle) and earthly reality (square).

- **Transformative Power**: Engaging with symbols, particularly those arising from the collective unconscious (archetypal symbols), can lead to profound psychological shifts and personal growth. They carry psychic energy (libido) that can be released and channeled for development.

- **Manifestation of the Numinous**: Symbols often point to something beyond rational understanding, evoking a sense of awe, mystery, or spiritual significance (the 'numinous'). This connects personal experience to universal patterns of meaning.

- **Individual and Universal**: While personal symbols emerge from individual experience, they often resonate with universal archetypal patterns, linking personal meaning to collective human themes.

Additional Concepts

The following concepts do not fit neatly into the previous sections, but they are essential building blocks for understanding the psyche from a Jungian perspective. They provide a foundational framework for how the psyche works and how we can approach our inner world.

The Principle of Opposites

All psychological life exists in a dynamic tension between opposing forces, and this tension is the primary source of psychic energy and development. This fundamental principle underscores the self-regulating nature of the psyche. Fundamental opposites include: Conscious/Unconscious, Progression/ Regression, Thinking/Feeling, and Extraversion/Introversion.

> **Example**: The tension between a conscious desire for security and an unconscious longing for adventure can create significant psychic energy, potentially leading to a new, more balanced life direction.

Final versus Causal

Jung emphasized a teleological (final) understanding of the psyche, which contrasts with a purely causal approach. A causal perspective explains current psychological states by tracing them back to past events or conditioning. In contrast, a final perspective understands psychological phenomena through their future goals, purposes, and potential for development.

Example - Causal: Explaining a person's anxiety by tracing it back to a traumatic childhood event.

Example - Final: Understanding a person's anxiety not just as a product of the past, but as a signal that the psyche is attempting to move towards a new stage of development or integrate a previously denied aspect, serving a future purpose.

Eros and Logos

Jung saw two fundamental principles driving human interaction and understanding. Logos is the principle of discrimination, consciousness, and rational analysis. It separates, analyzes, and creates meaning through logic. Eros is the principle of relationship, connection, and psychic relatedness. It binds, connects, and creates wholeness through relationship.

Example - Logos: A scientist meticulously dissecting a problem, breaking it down into components, and seeking objective truth through data.

Example - Eros: A therapist fostering empathy and connection within a group, helping individuals relate to each other's experiences to build community.

Anima and Animus

These are the archetypal representations of the opposite gender within the human psyche. The Anima is the unconscious feminine aspect in a man's personality, while the Animus is the unconscious masculine aspect in a woman's. The integration of these inner figures is crucial for psychological completeness. Once integrated, the anima and animus together form what is referred to as the syzygy (the divine couple), representing the union of opposing forces within the psyche.

Example - Anima: A man who is overly rational and emotionally reserved may have a dream of a beautiful, mysterious woman who challenges him to connect with his feelings and intuition. She represents his unintegrated Anima.

Example - Animus: A woman who is overly nurturing and focused on relationships may feel compelled by an inner voice to take a bold, independent action that goes against her usual nature. This voice represents her unintegrated Animus.

My Personal Application of Jung's Ideas

Now that we've mapped the psyche, as Jung saw it, and defined its core concepts, we can apply them. These aren't just abstract academic ideas; they are powerful tools for understanding the world inside us and outside of us. Jung's work was a product of his era, but it proves even more relevant today—not just for what it explains about the psyche but for what it can illuminate about our contemporary psychological reality.

The following are a few examples of applying Jung's concepts to contemporary life

The Shadow and Collective Shadow

In 1936, in his essay Wotan, Jung posited that the Nazi phenomenon was a massive eruption of the collective shadow. He saw it as an archetypal personification, the primordial Germanic god Wotan, that German society had repressed. The rational, civilized veneer cracked, and the primitive, destructive impulses constellated and emerged with terrifying power. The individual shadows of the citizens became amplified, co-opted, even possessed by the collective shadow. An entire nation acted out its darkest shadow impulses while believing it was pursuing a noble cause, all achieved without cellphones and digital infrastructure.

Jung's key concepts are even more impactful now than they were when he introduced them. Even with his prescience, he couldn't have conceived of our contemporary psychic landscape. Applying his theory of the collective shadow to our modern existence is illuminating.

The shadow is now profoundly transformed—more pervasive, more immediate, more restless, hyperconnected, more overwhelming. It lives on the device in your pocket—amplified by digital media through news sources that trade on impressions and seek to escalate outrage—separating and segmenting humanity with algorithms into ideological camps. In Jung's time, newspapers required intentional reading; radio broadcasts demanded deliberate listening. It was slower, allowing for time and space to reflect and process the material. Now —we scan. We superficially engage. We react off-the-hip through curated text, pictures, or video to earn emojis, replies, or reshares within our own echo chambers. Disagreements become amplified into full scale campaigns of vilification through hashtags. Critics labeled and tagged as pariahs. Thoughtful, reflective human discourse obliterated—we hate the offender and the offense equally. Individuation becomes individualization; ego as a brand; corporations as people; transformation as entertainment. The collective shadow's pernicious influence operates through its syntonic relationship with the individual shadow, allowing collective darkness to penetrate personal consciousness undetected. The collective shadow and the individual shadow have conflated into a deceptive, malignant hybrid—the mirrored self mistaking the reflection as the Self.

In this contemporary psychic landscape, the collective shadow is no longer a slumbering primordial god, awakened from a state of repression but a hyperactive, ubiquitous presence that infiltrates our personal lives with terrifying ease. Our hyperconnected reality has created the ideal conditions for the most insidious form of extraction: the subjugation of the self. As our individual identities are increasingly shaped by these external, algorithmically-driven reflections, we find ourselves losing touch with the authentic depths of our own being. This modern condition of profound internal disconnect, born from the conflation of the collective and individual shadows, is not just a psychological symptom—it is a pervasive state of being, one that requires its own diagnosis and its own path to reclamation.

Active Imagining, Amplification, and Constellation

Jung stressed the ethical obligation of engaging with the material gained from the unconscious through active imagining, which was to be brought back into conscious life and integrated. This process leads to a deeper understanding of oneself and a more congruent way of living. This material also provides a bridge to the greater human story of the collective. It helps one realize others have also had similar experiences.

Through active imagining, I've used amplification to access, constellate, and activate archetypal material. My unconscious provided vivid, visceral symbols that illustrate the psychic dimensions of these subjects. These symbols have proven to be indispensable in considering the psychic impact of various systems on my own psyche.

These symbols are not meant to be literal examples in any way. They don't dismiss the outright horror of the actual atrocities they reference, nor do they minimize their real and obvious physical, economic, or psychological impacts of these atrocities. Instead, they serve to illustrate the psychic dimensions of our contemporary systems.

Participation in our contemporary systems is paradoxically perceived as completely voluntary. However, on deeper introspection I've observed that the systems are actually internalized; they've been absorbed syntonically through the interplay between my individual shadow and the collective shadow. The tension between what Jung would refer to as the 'soul' and the system is the reason my unconscious chose the symbols it presents through active imagining. Surfacing uncomfortable truths through exaggerated symbols.

Here are some of my own symbols

- Shareholders as aristocracy

- Capitalism as colonialism

- Social media as brothel

- College as sharecropping

- Home-buying as tribal tribute system

- Celebrity as reliquary

- Social activism as guild membership

- Religion as vaudeville

- Politics as Broadway musical

- Corporate HR as plantation overseers

Activated Symbols

Through the process of amplification, what might seem like a mundane irritant is activated to expose deeper, unsettling tensions, constellating and providing symbolic material. For instance, you're not just "creating a spreadsheet for your company's annual report," you're "moving huge granite blocks to build a pyramid for your pharaoh." Similarly, "the great bank bailout of 2008" becomes "the first Thanksgiving, when indigenous tribes provided food to the colonizers —who would later decimate them."

This activation helps us to identify unconscious patterns through their exaggerated psychic charge. Once a complex or archetype activates, it will communicate to our consciousness through a symbol, then we are enabled to work with that symbol consciously and eventually integrate it.

Constellation

In Jungian terms, to constellate means to activate an archetype or a complex, causing it to emerge from the unconscious and manifest in consciousness. When a complex is constellated, it brings with it a powerful emotional charge and a cluster of related ideas and images or symbols. This activation can be triggered by an external event, an inner thought, active imagining, or a specific situation.

Through digital media, modern extractive systems are constantly constellating the collective shadow, triggering the activation of our darkest, most primitive psychological impulses on a mass—and excessively public—scale. We can see this unadorned in our social media feeds.

Amplification

Amplification is the process of enriching and deepening the meaning of a symbolic image from the unconscious by consciously connecting it to universal parallels. This is often done by relating a symbol from a dream or active imagination to similar images found in mythology, folklore, religion, art, and other cultural sources. The goal is to understand the symbol's universal significance, not just its personal meaning.

I propose that modern digital infrastructure—algorithms, social media, and news—acts as a literal engine of amplification. It takes a constellated emotion or idea and expands its power and influence exponentially, broadcasting it across a hyperconnected society. Disagreements, for example, are amplified into full-scale campaigns of vilification, turning a minor spark into a raging fire.

In short, the modern world constellates the shadows, and digital media amplifies them.

Constellated Archetypes

Constellation explains why archetypal patterns maintain such psychological weight in contemporary life. The universal patterns of hierarchy, submission, and extraction that were experienced through centuries of feudal domination, guild apprenticeships, and colonial relationships continue to be activated and reinforced through modern corporate structures, digital platforms, and economic systems. Each generation doesn't start fresh; they inherit archetypal patterns that have been continuously shaped and strengthened by similar extraction experiences across millennia. When a modern employee receives an urgent work email, they're not just responding to current corporate culture but accessing archetypal material about power, obedience, and survival that carries the accumulated psychological weight of countless individuals who faced similar dynamics throughout history. This is why seemingly minor contemporary situations can trigger disproportionate psychological responses—they're activating archetypal complexes that have been reinforced across generations of being conditioned for extraction.

The Dormant Soul Complex

...why a new complex?

It's an attempt to name the chronic general malaise felt by many in our contemporary existence. Something that manifests as a quiet disquiet, a core-deep exhaustion born from the psychic over-saturation, hyper-connectedness, and pervasive loss of meaning in our modern world. The soul goes dormant and vitality is stifled. This is not backed by clinical studies—it is based on personal observation. This is an opening for a discussion, not a closing commentary.

This state, which I refer to as the Dormant Soul Complex (DSC), isn't just another complex; it's an evolution of a complex. It is distinguished by its persistence and prevalence. Drawing from Jungian concepts, I assert that it arises from the nature of extractive systems that act upon our individual psyches through a syntonic relationship with the collective shadow. By way of this covert dynamic, the collective disarms our own soul's resistance to extraction. The tacit, unconscious subordination to extraction creates a nearly obsequious relationship to extractive systems and the general extractiveness of contemporary existence.

This systemic influence manifests at the individual level as a psychological configuration that systematically blocks one's connection to their authentic self, while preserving the ability to function externally and appear adaptive. The DSC operates as an autonomous complex—a 'splinter psyche'—that actively yet unconsciously prevents genuine Self-realization. It's what happens when the ego becomes chronically over-identified with persona structures or shadow projections, creating a sustained pattern where constructed identity actively prevents authentic psychological integration. Essentially, it creates an 'extracted self' that is more adept at navigating and existing within an extractive system than at living an authentic life. This 'extracted self' becomes the modern equivalent of the 'false self,' perfectly suited to a world that rewards external performance over internal truth.

Core Characteristics of the DSC

The Dormant Soul Complex manifests through a series of interlocking, self-reinforcing patterns that reveal the presence of the extracted self.

- **Pervasive Psychic Exhaustion**: A chronic state of soul-deep exhaustion born from the psychic over-saturation of modern existence. This exhaustion depletes the libidinal energy needed for authentic engagement with the world and for the deep, contemplative work of the psyche, leaving insufficient resources for transformation.

- **Persona as Extracted Self:** The social mask becomes so ingrained and dominant that it is mistaken for the entirety of one's being. The 'extracted self' is built from external inputs—social media validation, group affiliations, and a reliance on external metrics for worth—and is more a product of the extractive system than an expression of authentic selfhood. This confusion blocks access to deeper layers of the psyche and stifles individuation.

- **Archetypal Over-identification:** Instead of engaging with archetypes as dynamic, universal patterns, the individual clings to them as fixed, ready-made identities. This rigid over-identification with personas like 'the Victim,' 'the Trauma Survivor,' or 'The TechBro' provides a false sense of coherence and belonging, but it prevents the ego from engaging with the authentic Self.

- **Performance of Growth:** Inner work and personal development are externalized and commodified. The process of growth becomes a performance to be broadcast rather than a private, contemplative journey. This performative engagement paradoxically strengthens the ego-persona identity rather than dissolving it, leaving the individual with a sophisticated outward appearance of growth that lacks true Ego-Self integration.

DSC vs. Jung's Traditional Complex: The Systemic Difference

Jung saw a complex as an emotionally charged cluster that could serve as a pathway toward growth and wholeness. The DSC, however, represents what happens when the traditional, growth-oriented function of the complex is thwarted, and it is subverted by extractive, hyperconnected systems.

- **Libidinal Energy Depletion:** Extractive systems—through constant stimulation, attention farming, and a relentless pace—deplete the libidinal energy necessary for the contemplative work of engaging with complexes, leaving insufficient psychic resources for transformation.

- **Hyperconnected Reactivity**: The culture of 'react! react!!' eliminates the pause necessary for a response based on genuine self-reflection. Shadow projection becomes systematized onto anyone who isn't 'of our tribe,' preventing the integration work that traditional complexes could facilitate.

- **Systemic Reinforcement**: Rather than existing as isolated psychological phenomena, complexes within extractive systems become self-perpetuating patterns that make individuals complicit in maintaining the very conditions preventing their resolution.

- **Pace-Induced Stagnation**: The relentless speed of modern life prevents the slow, contemplative engagement that allows complexes to serve their traditional function as gateways to growth, instead trapping them in reactive loops.

Impact on the Individual and Collective Psyche

The presence of the DSC profoundly impacts the dynamic interplay between the collective and individual psyche, creating a state of psychic stagnation and distortion rather than the natural flow toward individuation.

- **Hyperconnected Distortion of Consciousness**: The relentless 'react! react!' culture of modern life filters authentic experience through the lens of persona maintenance. Our conscious awareness becomes rigidly focused on preserving a constructed social identity, preventing the ego from truly engaging with challenging insights from the unconscious.

- **Blocked Psyche and Stagnant Development**: The psyche, depleted of libidinal energy by extractive systems, becomes a site of blockage. Genuine transformative experiences are unconsciously filtered and reprocessed into familiar, ego-syntonic narratives, trapping the individual in repetitive, stagnant patterns and preventing the integration of their own unconscious material.

- **Commodified and Warped Collective Identity**: The DSC warps our relationship with the universal patterns of humanity. Instead of archetypes enriching our lives, we over-identify with them to bolster a false sense of self. The systematized shadow projection onto 'less evolved' others prevents us from recognizing the universal human patterns within ourselves, fueling division and conflict.

- **Stalled Individuation**: Perhaps the most critical impact is the DSC's active resistance to individuation. It is a sophisticated, unconscious defense mechanism that disrupts the natural, dynamic interplay between the individual and collective psyche. It creates a self that is adept at existing within extractive systems but is fundamentally alienated from its own soul and the deeper currents of collective human experience.

What the DSC Is Not

- A temporary psychological crisis or depression

- An existential crisis

- A simple addiction

- A conscious adaptation to difficult circumstances

- Normal ego development or persona formation

- A label to be applied to others for classification or separation

- A clinical pathology requiring a medical, psychiatric, or psychological diagnosis

The Extracted Self

So, what exactly is the 'extracted self'? To fully grasp the dynamics of the Dormant Soul Complex, we must look at its core psychological component: the extracted self. This is where psychological and sociological influences converge. It's a contemporary extension of the foundational ideas of the thinkers who first explored what it means to be disconnected from your authentic self.

Winnicott's True and False Self

At its core, the 'extracted self' functions as a pathological 'false self.' In his foundational work *The Maturational Processes and the Facilitating Environment* (1965), Donald Winnicott established the 'false self' as a defensive facade constructed in response to a threatening or non-responsive environment. In its pathological form, it completely obscures the 'true self,' leading to a 'profound absence of spontaneity and an inner experience of emptiness or deadness.' The 'extracted self' represents this defense in its most extreme and pervasive form, where the individual's psyche has built a sophisticated shell designed to navigate a world that is fundamentally perceived as unsafe or emotionally unresponsive. This defensive retreat of the authentic self is a direct parallel to the 'dormancy' described in the Dormant Soul Complex.

Jungian Analytical Psychology

The 'extracted self' is fundamentally an injury to the psyche. It is the direct consequence of the ego becoming chronically over-identified with the Persona —the social mask presented to the world. This over-identification, a 'neurotic narcissistic alienation,' prevents the ego from fulfilling its true function: mediating between the inner and outer worlds. Simultaneously, the Shadow—the disowned, unconscious parts of the self—is not integrated but is systematically projected onto the world, leading to a state of chronic externalized conflict.

Most critically, this dynamic represents a severe injury to the Ego-Self Axis, the vital connection between conscious awareness and the totality of the psyche. The 'dormant soul' is not merely a passive state of withdrawal but signifies the Self having become inert due to this prolonged lack of connection.

Object Relations and Self Psychology

These theories provide a relational context for the emergence of the extracted self. Object Relations Theory, particularly the concepts of 'splitting' and 'internalized bad objects,' shows how early relational failures can lead to a fragmented self. The extracted self could be seen as the psyche's ultimate defensive maneuver against this fragmentation, preferring to form a cohesive, external identity rather than engage with its splintered, internal object world. Self Psychology, as articulated in the defining works of Heinz Kohut, including *The Analysis of the Self* (1971), further explains the lack of vitality felt by the unactualized self. The pervasive emptiness and apathy described by Kohut directly parallel the psychic exhaustion of the DSC, suggesting that the 'dormancy' is a profound manifestation of sustained empathic failure on a societal scale.

Durkheim's Sociological Anomie

While the above theories explain the internal mechanisms, Émile Durkheim's concept of anomie provides the critical sociological backdrop. Anomie, as detailed in his seminal work *Suicide: A Study in Sociology* (1897), describes a state of normlessness and a breakdown of social bonds that leaves individuals feeling alienated and without purpose. The 'pervasive loss of meaning' and 'quiet disquiet' of the DSC are direct psychological symptoms of this societal condition. In an anomic world that offers no inherent meaning, the psyche—as a survival mechanism—constructs an identity from 'ready-made personality packages' and external validation. The 'extracted self' is the psychological response to a sociological void, a self built from the scraps of a broken collective consciousness.

The Call to Wholeness

The Dormant Soul Complex has been named, but it is not definitive. While our modern world is uniquely structured to create the 'extracted self,' the human psyche possesses a timeless, inherent drive toward wholeness. This drive is the very force that will guide the psyche out of its soul dormancy. The antidote to this pervasive malaise is not an external fix or a superficial solution. The path to reclaiming the soul, integrating the shadow, and realizing a life of authentic purpose lies in Jung's radical and timeless process of reclamation: **Individuation**.

Individuation

The Path of Reclamation

Jung's analytical psychology reveals a profound and inseparable connection between the individual and the collective psyche. The individual, with its conscious ego and personal unconscious, emerges from a deeper, universal foundation—the collective unconscious. This dynamic interplay is guided by the Self, the archetype of wholeness, and mediated by the transcendent function, which actively integrates our conscious and unconscious worlds.

His concepts aren't just theoretical; they offer a powerful framework for personal growth through the individuation process, leading to a more authentic, integrated, and purposeful life. This journey requires us to move beyond the limitations of our ego and societal conditioning. It is a path that, in this view, isn't just for personal gain, but for the collective evolution of the human species.

Jung's framework suggests that positive societal evolution depends on a critical mass of people realizing their true selves beyond societal conditioning.

The Profound Paradox of Individuation

Individuation presents a powerful paradox: it is a process of separating from the collective and opposing its norms, yet it paradoxically leads to a more intense and fulfilling relationship with it. True individuality is not achieved through isolation or mere eccentricity—which Jung termed individualism—but through integration of our universal human patterns and a differentiated relationship with societal norms. By becoming more genuinely ourselves, we are better equipped to participate meaningfully in and contribute to the collective, transforming our relationship from unconscious identification to purposeful engagement.

Remediation of the Dormant Soul Complex through Individuation

While the Dormant Soul Complex (DSC) names a contemporary psychic blockage, Jung's process of individuation provides a timeless roadmap for its remediation. It is the journey of becoming who you were always meant to be—a journey that directly addresses the malaise, fragmentation, and false identities of the DSC.

Navigating Individuation

The journey typically begins with the suffering of a life out of alignment. Either a pattern of the same challenging issues arising repeatedly or one life-altering event propelling us into a deeply troubling state. This suffering may act as a catalyst, prompting us to think differently and increase awareness. This catalyst has the potential to become our opportunity to set off on the journey of Individuation. A journey more spiralic than sequential in shape, where we encounter recurring themes and deepen our understanding of them with each turn—circumambulation.

Integrating the Shadow and Embracing Your Own Darkness

A hallmark of the DSC is our tendency to project our own repressed darkness onto others, labeling them as villains, and us as heroes. Individuation forces us to turn the gaze inward. It is the crucial stage of confronting and accepting the disowned parts of ourselves, the 'unfaced and unfelt parts of our psyche.'

When we bring these parts into awareness, we heal the source of our suffering and free ourselves from the constant need to blame others for our own internal struggles. This process isn't about becoming perfect; it's about learning to accept your imperfections and live with them deliberately.

The Emergence of Eudaimonic Sovereignty

With the integration of the shadow, a new capacity emerges: the ability to engage in honest relating. This is the first step toward Eudaimonic Sovereignty, a quality of embodied experience, a striving toward fulfillment. It is the capacity to participate meaningfully in both individual development and collective life without sacrificing either genuineness or connection. Eudaimonic Sovereignty is a continuous practice that unfolds throughout the individuation journey.

Consciously Managing the Persona

The DSC traps us in a performance of who we think we should be—a chronic over-identification with a social mask. One of the primary tasks of Individuation is the act of stripping that mask away. It's the process of differentiating from the collective, from its norms and expectations, to become the unique and genuine self hiding beneath the facade.

It isn't about living without a mask; it's about becoming a deliberate master of it, using it consciously as a flexible interface with the world, not as your total identity.

Integrating Opposites

This involves recognizing and integrating the fundamental polarities that exist within the psyche—Anima and Animus, Logos and Eros, thinking and feeling, structure and flow. The goal is not to eliminate these tensions but to develop the capacity to hold them consciously, allowing for a more complete and integrated personality.

Reclaiming the Transcendent Function

The DSC co-opts the transcendent function, twisting it to feed ego inflation and the thirst for status. Individuation reclaims this sacred process for its true purpose: to create new meaning and forge a path forward.

The transcendent function is the creative force that takes the tension between what we know and what we fear, between our conscious and unconscious worlds. It transmutes this tension into a new, uniting capacity that bridges opposites. By engaging deliberately in this process, we redirect our psychic energy away from ego-driven performance and toward genuine integration of the Self.

Fostering Authentic Development

The DSC presents us with a paradox: the more we chase 'growth' through external metrics and superficial performance, the more we strengthen the ego and the false self. Individuation is the opposite of this approach.

It is a natural, organic process of becoming, focused on growing into who you actually are, not who you think you should be. It pushes the boundaries of your self-perception and forces you to confront what you have refused to feel and what you have refused to know about yourself. This genuine journey is the key to overcoming the DSC.

Rediscovering Your Vocation

The pervasive emptiness and loss of meaning of the DSC can only be remedied by a deeper purpose. Jung called this 'vocation,' an 'irrational factor' that compels us to break free from the herd and its well-worn paths. It's an inner calling to unlock your unique destiny and achieve a sense of wholeness and fulfillment.

To find your vocation is to directly counteract the existential vacuum of the DSC and embark on a life of meaning and purpose.

From Individual Transformation to Collective Evolution

The DSC highlights the specific blockages of a psyche that has been conditioned for extraction. Individuation is the radical and timeless process of reclamation. By engaging deliberately with the totality of our psyche—the ego, persona, shadow, and Self—we can move beyond the 'extracted self' and begin the journey toward true psychological wholeness.

Yet Jung's vision of individuation extended beyond individual therapy to encompass a grander purpose. He suggested that individual psychological integration serves as a fundamental prerequisite for the positive evolution and transformation of the human species and society at large. The ultimate aim of individuation contributes to what he called the "collective evolution of a species."

Jung's framework implies that societal health is not merely a matter of political or economic structures but is deeply rooted in the psychological maturity of its individuals. This understanding elevates the importance of inner work to a collective imperative, establishing a direct link between the micro-level of individual psychological development and the macro-level of human civilization's progress.

Individuation and Eudaimonic Sovereignty

Building on Jung's framework, I introduce the concept of Eudaimonic Sovereignty, not as the goal of individuation, but as a natural consequence of it. Not as an achieved state but as a quality of embodied experience. The capacity to participate meaningfully in both individual development and collective life without losing either genuineness or connection.

This synthesis suggests that the ancient call to 'know thyself' carries profound implications not just for personal fulfillment, but for the future trajectory of human consciousness itself.

Part III |
A Path Forward

Individuation… then what?

Generative/ Regenerative Potential

For individuals who have emerged from the Dormant Soul Complex (DSC) through authentic individuation, a profound new dimension of development becomes accessible. It extends beyond personal wholeness to encompass collective flourishing. This represents a generative and regenerative potential, moving from individual psychological integration to a conscious, co-creative engagement with the broader world.

That potential evolution has three stages:

- **Eudaimonic Sovereignty** = individual

- **Koinonic Syntonomy** = individual + small group (collective)

- **Autonomic Synergeia** = small group (collective) + infrastructure of small groups (collectives)

Eudaimonic Sovereignty

- **Eudaimonia** (εὐδαιμονία): Literally 'good spirit' or 'good daemon.' It's often translated as 'happiness,' but in ancient Greek philosophy (especially Aristotle), it signifies a state of flourishing, living well, and achieving one's full potential, often through virtuous activity. It's an objective state of well-being, not merely subjective pleasure.

- **Sovereignty**: From Old French *soverain* (superior) via Latin *super* (above). While etymologically non-Greek, the concept of ultimate self-rule and authority within a domain resonates with Greek philosophical ideals of autonomous governance.

Eudaimonic Sovereignty is the state of being a self-ruling individual (sovereign) whose internal and relational existence is guided by an objectively good spirit and flourishing (eudaimonia). It encompasses conscious, authentic, and autonomous independence within one's interior psychological spaces and in relational contexts to others. This means having the genuine freedom to think, act, and experience in accordance with one's own inherent agency and highest good. It enables the Self to function through active, dynamic engagement with the wisdom of the soul—that which truly leads to flourishing, rather than being driven by fleeting egoic desires or unconscious shadow material. This 'good spirit' implies aligning with one's true nature and purpose, leading to a deeply fulfilling and virtuous life.

Eudaimonic Sovereignty is expressed through:

- Reclaiming personal agency and self-determination

- Developing internal authority and resilience

- Creating individual capacity for generative/regenerative action

- Breaking free from dependency relationships and transitioning to generative/ regenerative reciprocal relationships

Eudaimonic Sovereignty: The Liberated Individual

Scenario 1: Sara - The Awakened Professional

Sarah was a marketing executive who spent years climbing the corporate ladder, driven by external validation and societal expectations. After experiencing burnout and depression, she underwent a deep personal transformation process. Now embodying Eudaimonic Sovereignty, she:

- Reclaimed personal agency: Left her high-stress corporate job to start a values-aligned consulting practice focused on sustainable business practices

- Developed internal authority: Makes decisions based on her inner wisdom rather than external pressure or fear of judgment

- Created generative capacity: Uses her skills to help small businesses develop authentic brand stories that serve community needs

- Transitioned relationships: Moved from transactional networking to genuine reciprocal relationships built on mutual growth and support

Sarah no longer seeks validation through status or material accumulation. Instead, she experiences deep fulfillment through non-profit work that aligns with her authentic self and contributes meaningfully to others' wellbeing.

Scenario 2: Marcus - The Conscious Parent

Marcus grew up in a family system marked by emotional unavailability and conditional love. Through therapy and inner work, he achieved Eudaimonic Sovereignty and now:

- Exercises self-determination: Consciously chose to parent differently, breaking generational patterns of emotional neglect

- Maintains internal resilience: Responds to his children's challenges from a centered place rather than reactive patterns

- Demonstrates authentic agency: Makes parenting decisions based on what truly serves his children's development, not social expectations

- Models reciprocal relating: Shows his children how to maintain personal boundaries while being genuinely available and supportive

Marcus's sovereignty allows him to be fully present with his children while maintaining his own sense of self and purpose.

Scenario 3: Elena - The Liberated Artist

Elena spent decades trying to create art that would sell or gain critical acclaim, constantly adapting her vision to market demands and art world politics. After a period of creative crisis and soul-searching, she now embodies Eudaimonic Sovereignty through:

- Reclaimed creative authority: Creates work that emerges from her authentic inner vision rather than external expectations

- Developed financial resilience: Built diverse income streams that support her art without compromising her creative integrity

- Authentic self-expression: Uses her art to explore and express her deepest truths, regardless of popular trends

- Generative relationships: Collaborates with other artists from a place of mutual inspiration rather than competition or exploitation

Elena's art now carries a depth and power that comes from genuine self-expression, attracting an authentic audience that resonates with her work's integrity.

As individuals develop **Eudaimonic Sovereignty** they seek to co-create relationships with others, especially others who are also developing **Eudaimonic Sovereignty.** Through **Koinonic Syntonomy** they begin to organically self-organize into small-medium sized collaborative, generative/regenerative groups around collectively held goals or aspirations for group fulfillment.

Koinonic Syntonomy

- **Koinonia** (κοινωνία): Means 'fellowship,' 'joint participation,' 'sharing,' 'communion,' 'partnership,' or 'community.' It implies a deep, shared life and active engagement within a group.

- **Syntony** (συντονία): From *syn-* (together, with) and *tonos* (tension, pitch, tone). In psychology, it means being in 'harmony' or 'resonance' with one's environment, or being normally responsive to it. In its original sense, it implies a tuning together, a shared pitch or vibration.

Koinonic Syntonomy describes a small-to-medium-sized collective, group, or organizational structure comprised of Eudaimonically Sovereign individuals. The collective maintains its integrity through harmonious and resonant alignment (syntony) achieved by deep fellowship, joint participation, and shared purpose (koinonia) around common fulfillment, goals, or aspirations. The group operates through ethical, conscious, authentic, and generative/regenerative interrelation, where each individual's 'good spirit' contributes to the collective's harmonious resonance and shared well-being. It is an interdependent community tuned to a common frequency of flourishing.

Koinonic Syntonomy in practice:

- Facilitates transitions from internal Eudaimonic Sovereignty to relational co-creation in a small-to-medium group context through formation of collaborative, mutually-beneficial, and reciprocal relationships between individuals who are also developing Eudaimonic Sovereignty

- Encourages conscious, authentic, and autonomously aligned collective groups or dynamic organizational structures

- Enables organic self-organization into small generative/regenerative groups around collectively held goals or aspirations.

Koinonic Syntonomy: The Co-Creative Collective

Scenario 1: The Regenerative Farm Partnership

A group of eight Eudaimonically Sovereign individuals came together to create a regenerative agriculture project. Their Koinonic Syntonomy manifests as:

- Shared purpose alignment: All members are deeply committed to healing the land and providing healthy food to their community

- Harmonious decision-making: They use consensus processes that honor each person's sovereignty while maintaining group coherence

- Mutual support structures: When one member faces challenges, others provide support without creating dependency

- Collaborative resource sharing: Equipment, knowledge, and labor are shared based on need and capacity rather than transactional exchange

- Organic leadership: Leadership rotates naturally based on expertise and energy rather than hierarchical positions

The group maintains individual autonomy while creating something greater than any member could achieve alone: a thriving ecosystem that feeds both the land and the community.

Scenario 2: The Learning Community

Twelve families with school-age children formed a self-directed learning community that demonstrates Koinonic Syntonomy through:

- Joint participation in education: Parents with different expertise (science, arts, trades, etc.) share teaching responsibilities

- Resonant values alignment: All families are committed to child-led learning and holistic development

- Reciprocal support: Childcare, resources, and emotional support flow naturally based on family needs and capacities

- Community stewardship: Major decisions about curriculum and community direction are made through inclusive processes

- Individual sovereignty within community: Each family maintains their own approach while contributing to shared wellbeing

The children experience rich, diverse learning while parents create meaningful community bonds without sacrificing family autonomy.

Scenario 3: The Healing Arts Circle

Ten practitioners from various healing modalities (massage therapy, acupuncture, counseling, energy work, herbalism) formed a circle that embodies Koinonic Syntonomy:

- Shared mission resonance: All practitioners are aligned around holistic healing and serving their community's wellness

- Collaborative practice model: They share a beautiful healing center, refer clients to each other, and co-create wellness programs

- Resource synergy: Pool resources for education, equipment, and marketing while maintaining individual practice sovereignty

- Peer support network: Regular gatherings for case consultation, skill sharing, and mutual support in their healing work

- Emergent programming: Community workshops and events arise organically from the group's unified inspiration and community needs

Each practitioner maintains their unique approach and client relationships while benefiting from the wisdom, support, and enhanced capacity of the circle.

As these organically self-organized small groups mature, they begin to use **Autonomic Synergeia** to further organize more broadly with other groups/ collectives to create generative/regenerative infrastructures.

Autonomic Synergeia

- **Autonomic** (αὐτόνομος): From *autos* (self) and *nomos* (law, custom). Meaning 'self-governing' or 'living under one's own laws.'

- **Synergeia** (συνεργία): From *syn-* (together, with) and *ergon* (work). Meaning 'working together,' 'cooperation,' or 'joint effort.' It implies a combined action where the whole is greater than the sum of its parts.

Autonomic Synergeia refers to the dynamic coordination and responsive interplay of Eudaimonically Sovereign individuals, organized into Koinonically Syntonomic groups, who are self-governing (autonomic) and working together collaboratively (synergeia) to create self-regulating generative/regenerative infrastructures at the societal level. This infrastructure operates through harmonious, intentional, and transparent self-regulation and self-refinement, fostering a societal system where collective effort amplifies individual flourishing, and the entire structure functions according to its own inherent, beneficial principles. It is a society where the combined 'work' of self-governing, flourishing communities leads to an emergent, self-sustaining greater good.

Autonomic Synergeia would facilitate:

153

- Distributed power that regenerates rather than extracts

- Collective coordination that enhances rather than diminishes individual agency

- Self-Regulating emergent societal network structures that create collective abundance and opportunities for fulfillment rather than competition and scarcity created by resource hoarding and upward aggregation

- Shared emergent governance that grows everyone's capacity through continuous co-creation and refinement

Autonomic Synergeia: The Regenerative Society

Scenario 1: The Bioregional Network

Multiple Koinonically Syntonomic groups across a bioregion (watershed area) have developed Autonomic Synergeia, creating:

- Distributed resource networks: The farm collective, learning community, maker spaces, and healing arts collectives share resources and coordinate activities

- Self-regulating governance: Regional decisions emerge through networked councils where each group maintains autonomy while contributing to bioregional wellbeing

- Regenerative economics: Local currencies, bartering, and gift economies operate alongside traditional markets, keeping wealth circulating locally

- Ecological restoration: Coordinated efforts to restore watersheds, forests, and soil health benefit the entire region

- Cultural renaissance: Shared festivals, skill-sharing events, and collaborative art projects strengthen social bonds across groups

This network demonstrates how shared abundance emerges when self-governing groups work together without sacrificing individual or group sovereignty.

Scenario 2: The Urban Regeneration Movement

Multiple neighborhoods within a city have developed interconnected networks exhibiting Autonomic Synergeia:

- Neighborhood sovereignty: Each area maintains its unique character while participating in city-wide coordination

- Resource circulation: Tool libraries, community gardens, skill shares, and care networks operate across neighborhood boundaries

- Emergent governance: City-wide decisions emerge from neighborhood councils working in dynamic collaboration with municipal government

- Economic transformation: Community-owned businesses, cooperative housing, and participatory budgeting reduce extraction and increase local wealth

- Infrastructure cooperation: Renewable energy microgrids, composting systems, and transportation networks are collaboratively managed

Individual residents maintain personal sovereignty, neighborhoods preserve their unique identities, and the city becomes a model of regenerative urban living.

Scenario 3: The Professional Network Ecosystem

Dozens of professional partnerships across various industries (design, technology, consulting, trades, wellness, education) have formed an interconnected ecosystem demonstrating Autonomic Synergeia:

- Cross-industry collaboration: Different partnerships share expertise and resources for complex projects that require diverse skills

- Regenerative business practices: All participating groups operate on principles that enhance rather than extract from their communities

- Distributed economic flows: Revenue, resources, and opportunities circulate throughout the network based on capacity and need

- Shared learning infrastructure: Common educational platforms, mentorship programs, and innovation labs benefit all network members

- Self-organizing governance: Network-wide decisions emerge through representative councils while preserving each partnership's autonomy

- Systemic impact: The network's unified influence creates positive changes in industry standards and practices

This professional ecosystem demonstrates how economic activity can become truly regenerative when organized through collaborative sovereignty rather than competitive extraction.

The Post-Individuation Journey in Practice

The journey from individual integration to collective flourishing begins not with grand gestures, but with small, conscious actions. This framework is not a passive ideal but a living practice. Here are some tangible steps for putting the principles of Eudaimonic Sovereignty, Koinonic Syntonomy, and Autonomic Synergeia into action.

Cultivating Eudaimonic Sovereignty

Before you can co-create, you must be truly sovereign. The first stage is an internal journey of reclaiming your own authority.

- **Practice Authentic Self-Inquiry**: Commit to a regular practice of journaling, meditation, or inner work. Ask yourself, "What are my deepest values?" and "What truly brings me a sense of purpose and flourishing, independent of external validation?"

- **Identify and Unpack Your Dependencies**: Notice where you seek validation, security, or identity from external sources—your job, social media, a relationship, or even a political group. Begin to consciously shift your reliance from these external structures to your own internal wisdom.

- **Establish Energetic Boundaries**: Learn to say 'no' to commitments that drain your energy or don't align with your highest good. This is a powerful act of self-determination.

Co-Creating Koinonic Syntonomy

With a foundation of individual sovereignty, you can now seek out and build resonant communities.

- **Seek Out Resonant Partnerships**: Intentionally seek personal, professional, and creative relationships with others who are also on the path of authentic self-discovery. Prioritize mutual growth over transactional benefit.

- **Practice Conscious Communication**: In group settings, focus on expressing your authentic truth from a place of sovereignty rather than reactivity. Learn to listen deeply to others without taking on their emotional burdens or trying to 'fix' them.

- **Form Small, Purpose-Aligned Groups**: Begin with a small collective of trusted individuals around a shared passion or goal, such as a book club, a skill-sharing circle, a community garden project, or a creative collective. Experiment with non-hierarchical decision-making.

Building Autonomic Synergeia

As you find your place in small, harmonious groups, the next step is to connect with other groups to build a larger regenerative infrastructure.

- **Network with Other Collectives**: Actively map and connect with other Koinonically Syntonomic groups in your area or field. Look for opportunities to share resources, knowledge, and labor.

- **Co-Create Shared Systems**: Join or help create shared infrastructure like local tool libraries, community-owned businesses, or cooperative housing. Focus on projects that create collective abundance for everyone involved.

- **Engage in Emergent Governance**: Participate in local or regional councils that use consensus and collaboration to solve problems. This is about working with, not against, others to solve complex challenges.

Principles of the Integrated System

I assert that these three levels would function as an integrated system where each tier both depends upon and supports the others. As individuals develop Eudaimonic Sovereignty, they naturally seek resonant community—Koinonic Syntonomy; as these communities mature, they organically create regenerative infrastructure—Autonomic Synergeia—and as infrastructure emerges, it provides the conditions for deeper individual and collective flourishing. This creates a sustainable spiral of generative development that contrasts sharply with the unsustainable degeneration of extractive systems.

This post-individuation journey, culminating in Autonomic Synergeia, represents a powerful alternative to current 'extractive systems' which contribute to the Dormant Soul Complex. This speculative evolution represents a societal transformation driven by integrated individuals and co-creative collectives, leading to a truly regenerative human civilization.

Key Characteristics Across All Levels

While Eudaimonic Sovereignty, Koinonic Syntonomy, and Autonomic Synergeia represent distinct levels of development, they are all governed by a shared set of underlying principles. These key characteristics act as a common blueprint, ensuring that the entire system remains generative, regenerative, and true to its purpose of fostering flourishing. They are the essential conditions that distinguish this developmental spiral from the unsustainable dynamics of extractive systems.

The preceding scenarios illustrate how personal liberation naturally evolves into collective flourishing by allowing individuals to maintain their sovereignty while choosing conscious collaboration.

What Makes These Scenarios Work:

- **Foundation in sovereignty**: Each level builds on individuals who have done their inner work and reclaimed authentic agency

- **Voluntary participation**: No coercion or manipulation, all engagement is chosen freely

- **Dynamic responsiveness**: Structures adapt organically to changing needs and circumstances

- **Reciprocal benefit**: Everyone involved experiences genuine enhancement of their capacity and wellbeing

- **Regenerative impact**: Activities restore and enhance the health of people, communities, and ecosystems

What Is NOT Represented by These Scenarios:

- **Communes or intentional communities**—which often require individuals to subordinate personal sovereignty

- **Traditional cooperatives**—which may lack the depth of personal transformation required

- **Political movements**—which typically focus on changing external structures rather than inner development

- **Utopian fantasies**—these are practical approaches that can begin immediately with committed individuals. They require effort; they are not magic solutions.

Personal Agency. Collective Flourishing.

The post-individuation journey outlined in this chapter is more than a theoretical framework; it is a proposed living model for human and societal evolution. It begins with a fundamental choice: to move beyond the limitations of extractive systems and commit to a sustainable spiral of generative development.

The journey from Eudaimonic Sovereignty to Autonomic Synergeia is a path of conscious collaboration. It contends that personal liberation is not an end in itself, but the essential prerequisite for building true community and regenerative infrastructure. These three levels are not separate destinations but an integrated, dynamic system where each layer both depends upon and strengthens the others.

The path forward is not a political movement or a utopian fantasy, but a personal act an individual may take in the interest of contributing to a collective reality. A practical, immediate choice to engage in inner work, seek out resonant partnerships, and co-create shared systems. Through these deliberate actions, we can move from merely surviving to genuinely flourishing, transforming not only ourselves but the very fabric of human civilization.

Conclusion

The Integrated Psyche and Human Evolution

This exploration began with a fundamental question: how do systems of extraction persist across vastly different historical contexts? Through the Architecture, Model, and Facets framework, we traced the evolution of extractive mechanisms from the overt bondage of Medieval feudalism to the subtle psychological coercions of contemporary corporate culture. While the methods have evolved—from bailiffs collecting taxes to 'culture of urgency' demanding constant availability—the underlying architecture remains remarkably consistent: the concentration of power and resources through hierarchical control.

The framework revealed a crucial insight: modern extraction has become increasingly psychological and internalized. Where Medieval peasants understood their bondage explicitly, today's workers face 'hustle culture' that disguises self-extraction as self-actualization, making resistance feel like personal failure rather than systemic critique. The very systems that drain our resources, time, and well-being present themselves as opportunities for growth and success.

This analysis exposed not just the mechanics of extraction, but its profound psychological impact. The persistent patterns of hierarchy and control embed themselves in the collective unconscious, creating what I have identified as the Dormant Soul Complex—a contemporary psychic configuration that systematically blocks authentic self-realization while maintaining the appearance of adaptation and success.

Yet understanding the problem is only the beginning. The persistence of extractive systems across centuries suggests they operate at a level deeper than conscious awareness—embedded in the very structures of the collective psyche. This is where Jung's analytical psychology becomes not just relevant, but essential.

Jung's framework reveals how extractive systems perpetuate themselves through psychological mechanisms: shadow projection, persona identification, and the co-opting of the transcendent function for ego inflation rather than genuine integration. The Dormant Soul Complex emerges as a modern manifestation of these ancient patterns, creating what we might call an 'extracted self'—perfectly adapted to navigating extractive environments but fundamentally disconnected from authentic purpose and meaning.

The traditional Jungian process of individuation offers a direct path through this psychological maze. By confronting the shadow, consciously managing the persona, integrating opposites, and reclaiming the transcendent function, individuals can break free from the internalized patterns that keep them trapped in cycles of extraction and performance.

But individuation is more than personal liberation—it's the foundation for generative living. As individuals reclaim their authentic capacity for meaning-making, creative engagement, and genuine relationship, they naturally begin to participate in life differently. They seek resonant partnerships, co-create regenerative systems, and contribute to collective abundance rather than scarcity.

This individual transformation opens the door to what we have termed the post-individuation journey: a progression from personal Eudaimonic Sovereignty through collaborative Koinonic Syntonomy to societal Autonomic Synergeia. This isn't utopian thinking—it's the natural consequence of individuals who have reclaimed their psychological wholeness choosing to engage collectively from a place of authentic agency rather than unconscious reactivity.

Eudaimonic Sovereignty represents the capacity to participate consciously in both individual development and collective life without sacrificing authenticity or connection. When enough individuals embody this quality, they naturally seek out others with similar depth and intentionality, creating the conditions for Koinonic Syntonomy—groups that function through genuine collaboration rather than hierarchical control. These regenerative partnerships, in turn, become the building blocks for Autonomic Synergeia: societal structures that operate through distributed power, enhanced individual agency, and collective abundance.

Jung's vision extends far beyond individual therapy to encompass what he called the "collective evolution of a species." He believed that positive societal evolution depends on a "critical mass of people realizing their true selves beyond societal conditioning." Our framework suggests that this critical mass is not an abstract ideal but a practical possibility—one that emerges naturally when individuals complete the work of psychological integration and begin to participate in life from their authentic ground.

As Jung emphasized, "the sole purpose of human existence is to kindle a light of meaning in the darkness of mere being." My hope is that this journey from extractive systems through individuation to generative collective life represents a kindling—not just personal meaning, but the illumination of new possibilities for human civilization itself.

In Closing

I leave this now to you, the reader. It bears restating…

This is not a manifesto. It is intended to be a mirror.
It is not a dogma. It is meant to be a tool.

It is proposed as the opening of a conversation, not the conclusion of a monologue.

This personal framework comes from my synthesis of conceptual, philosophical, and academic materials, combined with my introspective conversations with that material: a nearly-three-decade-long conversation created an analytical lens used to observe and articulate the lived experience.

My aspirations for publishing this personal conceptual framework are simple: name the 'thing' and its 'ecosystem'; use historical examples methodically and rigorously to share clues about its origin; then propose a vision for a way forward.

I release my conceptual framework along with its optimistic future vision. This is speculative social philosophy. It's born from deeply interdisciplinary thinking, but it is only one person's perspective.

I'm not advocating for torches, pitchforks, and guillotines... but instead... a zafu and a good Jungian therapist. Heal thyself to heal civilization.

Is this conceptual framework logical? ...or just a complex, bloated recursive system of useless synthesis that happens to include a few references to Marx and Jung? Is it too broad? Too deep? Too interdisciplinary? Does it stand on its own merit? ...or does it fade into oblivion? Is it visionary work or the artifact of an armchair wannabe scholar's delusion? Is it optimistic iconoclasm pragmatically applied or lofty utopian idealism?

You decide. I leave those answers to you, the individual reader, and to the collective world at large.

So, let's say you're eudaimonically sovereign... what's next? What does a generative/regenerative life look like to you?

Additional Reading

This list is not exhaustive.

'*' = Essential reading

Adorno, Theodor W.

Dialectic of Enlightenment (1944, with Max Horkheimer)

The Authoritarian Personality (1950, with Else Frenkel-Brunswik, Daniel J. Levinson, and R. Nevitt Sanford)

Negative Dialectics (1966)

de Beauvoir, Simone

She Came to Stay (1943)

The Second Sex (1949)

Blake, William

The Marriage of Heaven and Hell (1790)

Songs of Innocence and of Experience (1794)

Visions of the Daughters of Albion (1793)

Bloch, Ernst

The Spirit of Utopia (1918)

The Principle of Hope (1954-1959, three-volume series)

Bly, Robert

A Little Book on the Human Shadow (1988)

Iron John: A Book About Men (1990)

More Than True: The Wisdom of Fairy Tales (1999)

Campbell, Joseph

The Hero with a Thousand Faces (1949)

Myths to Live By (1972)

The Power of Myth (1988)

The Masks of God (1959-1968, four-volume series)

Coelho, Paulo

The Alchemist (1988)

Veronika Decides to Die (1998)

The Devil and Miss Prym (2000)

The Archer (2020)

Durkheim, Émile

The Division of Labour in Society (1893)

Suicide: A Study in Sociology (1897)

Foucault, Michel

Madness and Civilization (1961)

The Order of Things (1966)

Discipline and Punish: The Birth of the Prison (1975)

von Franz, Marie-Louise

The Interpretation of Fairy Tales (1970)

The Problem of the Puer Aeternus (1970)

Shadow and Evil in Fairy Tales (1974)

Alchemy: An Introduction to the Symbolism and the Psychology (1980)

On Divination and Synchronicity: The Psychology of Meaningful Chance (1980)

The Collected Works of Marie-Louise von Franz (2021 —, multiple volumes)

Heidegger, Martin

Being and Time (1927)

Introduction to Metaphysics (1935)

Basic Writings (1977)

Henderson, Joseph

The Wisdom of the Serpent: The Myths of Death, Rebirth, and Resurrection (1963)

Thresholds of Initiation (1967)

Shadow and Self: Selected Papers in Analytical Psychology (1990)

Hillman, James

The Myth of Analysis: Three Essays in Archetypal Psychology (1972)

Re-Visioning Psychology (1975)

The Dream and the Underworld (1979)

The Soul's Code: In Search of Character and Calling (1996)

A Terrible Love of War (2004)

The Uniform Edition of the Writings of James Hillman (2004-2021, multiple volumes)

   The Uniform Edition of the Writings of James Hillman, Book 1: Archetypal Psychology

   The Uniform Edition of the Writings of James Hillman, Book 2: City and Soul

   The Uniform Edition of the Writings of James Hillman, Book 4: From Types to Images

   The Uniform Edition of the Writings of James Hillman, Book 6: Mythic Figures

hooks, bell

Ain't I a Woman?: Black Women and Feminism (1981)

Feminist Theory: From Margin to Center (1984)

All About Love: New Visions (2000)

Johnson, Robert A.

He: Understanding Masculine Psychology (1974)

She: Understanding Feminine Psychology (1977)

We: Understanding the Psychology of Romantic Love (1983)

Owning Your Own Shadow: Understanding the Dark Side of the Psyche (1991)

Jung, C.G. (Carl Gustav)

Memories, Dreams, Reflections (1962)

Man and His Symbols (1964)

The Red Book: Liber Novus (2009)

The Collected Works of C.G. Jung (2014, multiple volumes. New Critical Editions, expected 2026.)

Collected Works of C. G. Jung, Volume 5: Symbols of Transformation

Collected Works of C. G. Jung, Volume 8: The Structure and Dynamics of the Psyche

The Collected Works of C. G. Jung, Volume 9, Part 1: Archetypes and the Collective Unconscious

Collected Works of C. G. Jung, Volume 9, Part 2: Aion: Researches into the Phenomenology of the Self

Collected Works of C. G. Jung, Volume 10: Civilization in Transition

Collected Works of C. G. Jung, Volume 11: Psychology and Religion: West and East

Collected Works of C. G. Jung, Volume 12: Psychology and Alchemy

Collected Works of C. G. Jung, Volume 13: Alchemical Studies

Collected Works of C. G. Jung, Volume 14: Mysterium Coniunctionis

Collected Works of C. G. Jung, Volume 15: Spirit in Man, Art, And Literature

Collected Works of C. G. Jung, Volume 18: The Symbolic Life: Miscellaneous Writings

Encountering Jung (multiple volumes)

Jung on Active Imagination (1997, Encountering Jung Series, Edited and Introduced by Joan Chodrow)

Jung on the Hudson (multiple volumes)

Jung and the Alchemical Imagination (2000, Jung on the Hudson Series, author: Jeffrey Raffe)

Healing the Wounded God: Finding Your Personal Guide to Individuation and Beyond (2002, Jung on the Hudson Series, authors: Jeffrey Raffe and Linda Bonnington Vocatura)

The Practice of Ally Work: Meeting and Partnering with Your Spirit Guide in the Imaginal World (2006, Jung on the Hudson Series, author: Jeffrey Raffe)

Kalsched, Donald

The Inner World of Trauma: Archetypal Defenses of the Personal Spirit (1996)

Trauma and the Soul: A Psycho-Spiritual Approach to Human Development and its Interruption (2013)

The Soul and the Symptom (2018)

Kierkegaard, Søren

Either/Or (1843)

Fear and Trembling (1843)

The Sickness Unto Death (1849)

Koestler, Arthur

The Ghost in the Machine (1967)

Kohut, Heinz

The Analysis of the Self (1971)

van der Kolk, Bessel

Psychological Trauma (1987)

*Traumatic Stress: The Effects of Overwhelming Experience on Mind, Body, and Society (1996)

*The Body Keeps the Score: Brain, Mind, and Body in the Healing of Trauma (2014)

Marcuse, Herbert

*Eros and Civilization (1955)

*One-Dimensional Man (1964)

Marx, Karl

*The Communist Manifesto (1848, with Friedrich Engels)

*Capital (Das Kapital), Volumes 1-3 (1867-1894)

Maté, Gabor

When the Body Says No: The Cost of Hidden Stress (2003)

In the Realm of Hungry Ghosts: Close Encounters with Addiction (2008)

*The Myth of Normal: Trauma, Illness, and Healing in a Toxic Culture (2022)

Meade, Michael

*Fate and Destiny: The Two Agreements of the Soul (2008)

Why the World Doesn't End: Tales of Renewal in Times of Loss (2012)

*The Genius Myth: How to Take Yourself Seriously (2020)

Mumford, Lewis

Technics and Civilization (1934)

The City in History: Its Origins, Its Transformations, and Its Prospects (1961)

The Myth of the Machine (1967-1970, two volumes)

Nietzsche, Friedrich

Thus Spoke Zarathustra (1883)

Beyond Good and Evil (1886)

On the Genealogy of Morality (1887)

Perel, Esther

Mating in Captivity: Unlocking Erotic Intelligence (2006)

The State of Affairs: Rethinking Infidelity (2017)

Roszak, Theodore

The Making of a Counter Culture: Reflections on the Technocratic Society and Its Youthful Opposition (1969)

Where the Wasteland Ends: Politics and Transcendence in Postindustrial Society (1972)

Person/Planet: The Creative Disintegration of Industrial Society (1978)

Shaw, Martin

A Branch from the Lightning Tree: Ecstatic Myth and the Grace of Wildness (2011)

Scatterlings: Getting Claimed in the Anishinaabe Way (2014)

Courting the Wild Twin (2020)

Bard Skull (2023)

Singer, Thomas and Kimbles, Samuel

The Cultural Complex: Contemporary Jungian Perspectives on Psyche and Society (2004)

The Vision Thing: Myth, Politics and Psyche in the World (2014)

Cultural Complexes and the Soul of America: Myth, Psyche, and Politics (2020)

Stein, Murray

In Midlife: A Jungian Perspective (1983)

Jung's Map of the Soul (1998)

The Principle of Individuation: Toward the Development of Human Consciousness (2006)

Vervaeke, John

Zombies in Western Culture: A Twenty-First Century Crisis (2017)

Awakening from the Meaning Crisis (2021)

Mentoring the Machines: Orientation - Part One (2024)

Whitman, Walt

Leaves of Grass (1855)

Winnicott, Donald

The Maturational Processes and the Facilitating Environment (1965)

Woodman, Marion

Addiction to Perfection: The Still Unravished Bride (1982)

The Pregnant Virgin: A Process of Psychological Transformation (1985)

*Leaving My Father's House: A Journey to Conscious Femininity (1992)

*The Maiden King: The Reunion of Masculine and Feminine (1998, with Robert Bly)

Bone: Dying and the Sacred Feminine (2000)

Zuboff, Shoshana

In the Age of the Smart Machine: The Future of Work and Power (1988)

*The Age of Surveillance Capitalism: The Fight for a Human Future at the New Frontier of Power (2019)